Trusting Readers

Trusting Readers

Powerful Practices for Independent Reading

Jennifer Scoggin *and* Hannah Schneewind

Heinemann
Portsmouth, NH

Heinemann
145 Maplewood Avenue, Suite 300
Portsmouth, NH 03801
www.heinemann.com

Offices and agents throughout the world

Library of Congress Control Number: 2021934230
ISBN: 978-0-325-12047-8

Editor: Zoë Ryder White
Production Editor: Kimberly Capriola
Cover and Interior Designer: Vita Lane
Illustrator: Anzia Anderson
Typesetter: Gina Poirier Design
Manufacturing: Val Cooper

Printed in the United States of America on acid-free paper
1 2 3 4 5 MPP 25 24 23 22 21
April 2021 Printing

To my parents
—*H.S.*

To my favorite readers,
Lily and Charlie
—*J.S.*

Contents

6

Trust Readers to Do the Work: The Impact Conference

118

7

Trusting Time: You Can Do a Lot in 180 Days

142

Online Resource
Contents

Visit **Hein.pub/TrustingReaders** to access these Companion Online Resources.

Acknowledgments

Pam and Jim Allyn, thank you for being such great matchmakers and putting us together years ago. This idea was born on a train ride into New York City, headed to LitLife, and since then has grown in classrooms, on planes, during car rides, on conference room floors, and in all corners of our homes.

Dorothy Barnhouse, thank you for collaborating, thinking, and chatting with us and for your brilliant work centered on listening to children.

Ellin Keene, we may never get over the magnitude of having you read, comment on, and support our work on reading engagement. Thank you for your seminal work!

To the students and teachers at Niantic Center School, the Country School, and Highland Park Elementary School, thank you for sharing your reading lives with us and trusting us to give all this a go!

Margaret LaRaia, thank you for believing in us from the start. Your wisdom and collaboration shaped this project in immeasurable ways.

To our editor, Zoë Ryder White, your expertise as a teacher and writer was invaluable. In moments of panic or uncertainty, one phone call or bit of feedback from you allowed us to take a breath and imagine new spaces of possibility for this work.

Anzia Anderson, your illustrations are a gift! They perfectly capture the feeling of a trusting, joyful relationship between teacher and student.

To the entire team at Heinemann, thank you for bringing our book to life so beautifully! We feel grateful for your commitment to our vision. You are the loveliest folks around.

—Jen and Hannah

Robin Trainor, my education professor at Vassar, you shared your infectious love of early literacy, which inspired me to teach first grade and taught me the value of kidwatching.

Peter Heaney and Liz Phillips at PS 321, you trusted a first-year teacher. Liz, you and I spent countless hours wondering and teaching together. Your boundless positivity and endless faith in all students stay with me always. Starting my teaching life at PS 321, surrounded by thoughtful teachers, was a gift.

Lucy Calkins, it is your voice I hear in my head when I sit next to children and teachers.

Kathy Collins, colleague and friend, I love your sense of humor and your instincts about children.

Members of the original reading think tank, especially Kathleen Tolan, and the entire Teachers College Reading and Writing Project, I grew up as a teacher with you.

Carl Anderson, friend and mentor, thank you for listening to me and saying, "This is a book." Everything that I know about conferring, I know from you. I am grateful for your many writing conferences during all stages of this book.

Jen Serravallo, thank you for trusting me to share your magical work with teachers. This book grew out of your books.

Amy Ludwig VanDerwater, thank you for sitting next to me at dinner at NCTE in 2017 and asking me what I was currently writing.

Teachers in Manchester, Connecticut, Marquardt District 15, and PS 321, thank you for your feedback and for trusting me to work with your students.

Jen, thank you for being an amazing thought partner, writing partner, and friend. Thank you for trusting me to bring our work into the world together.

Thank you to my sister Rachel for always asking, "How's the book going?"

A special thank-you to my sister Sarah, who never stopped asking, "When are you going to write a book?"

And most importantly to my family, Nick, Elizabeth, James, and Sebastian: thank you for always encouraging me, even when it meant that I missed family dinners. I love you.

—Hannah

Years ago, in college, when I first thought that just maybe I wanted to be a teacher, Bud O'Connor showed me the value of joy, laughter, and play. From the moment I set foot in *his* classroom, I never looked back.

To my first team of amazing colleagues, Elizabeth Keat, Lauren McMullan, Susan West, Michelle Kelly, Jyoti Parekh, and Julie Dulay: working with you taught me how to trust and be trusted as a teacher.

Pam and Jim Allyn, thank you for teaching me to trust myself in this work. You have always believed in and supported my work, pushing me to take leaps even before I thought I was ready myself.

To all the teachers who have welcomed me into their classrooms, thank you for trusting me with your students.

Hannah, I tell everyone you are the best thing to happen to me in my forties. Our friendship and collaboration is a master class in trust. I couldn't ask for a better partner or friend.

Thank you, Mom, for being the best teacher I have ever had.

And to Nathan, Lily, and Charlie, thank you for standing behind me every step of the way, trusting that this was worth it. I love you.

—Jen

For every WHAT IF,
the imagination creates a possibility,
and in that possibility
lives a story.

—Rebecca Kai Dotlich

Introduction ——————————————————

[Collective teacher efficacy] is the combined belief that it is us that causes learning . . . because when you fundamentally believe you can make the difference and then you feed it with the evidence . . . then that is dramatically powerful.

—John Hattie

What if we realized the best way to ensure an effective educational system is not by standardizing our curricula and tests but by standardizing the opportunities available to all students?

—Ibram X. Kendi

Imagination is what, above all, makes empathy possible. It is what enables us to cross the empty spaces between ourselves and those we teachers have called "other" over the years. If those others are willing to give us clues, we can look in some manner through strangers' eyes and hear through their ears. That is because, of all our cognitive capacities, imagination is the one that permits us to give credence to alternative realities. It allows us to break with the taken for granted, to set aside familiar distinctions and definitions.

—Maxine Greene

Literacy is not just about reading words on the page; it also carries some sort of action. In other words, reading and writing are transformative acts that improve self and society.

—Gholdy Muhammad

We were halfway through writing this book when the coronavirus pandemic erupted and disrupted all of our lives. Suddenly, teachers who loved seeing children every day had to jump into remote learning with little or no time to prepare. During this time, teachers quickly realized the power of staying connected. Everyone craved the oft taken-for-granted connections that were part of everyday life—the thumbs-up from the school bus driver, the smile from an administrator as children walked through the front door, and, of course, the irreplaceable connection between teachers and students and between students themselves. Although we missed conferring with readers in person, our work—harnessing the power of connections—began to feel timelier than ever.

And yet, as we begin to revalue the importance of connections, we also must confront the inequities that were made so painfully clear during this same time. The Black Lives Matter movement shines a light on the institutional racism that has plagued our country, including our school system, resulting in inequitable opportunities and uneven access to the high-quality education that all students deserve. As educators, it is our responsibility to move beyond acknowledgment of these issues and shift toward the critical conversations and reflective honesty necessary to become agents of change. Connecting with, imagining possibilities for, and bolstering the strengths of all readers with impactful instruction is our contribution.

An Invitation to Teachers

In the rush to collect data, cover curriculum, and write report cards, all while managing a class full of unique personalities (in person or remotely), it can be easy to lose sight of the values that brought us to the classroom in the first place. Years ago, we sat with Maxine Greene in her salon as she reflected on her years of experience in education. In her eighties at the time, she stated simply, "I am who I am not yet," positioning herself and her work in the field as always existing in a state of becoming. There is always possibility beyond where we are in the current moment. What experiences do you want to create for your students as readers? What professional goals do you want to set for yourself? What values do you want to bring into focus in your work?

We invite you to consider your own practice and imagine new spaces of possibility for your readers, the teaching of reading, and the purpose of education. Because of COVID-19 and the resulting global health crisis, education has been disrupted, creating a space for us to not just gesture toward reforming schools but start over with the power of centering trust, teacher autonomy, and equitable literacy practices. If there is to be any silver lining to this moment in history, let it be that teachers had a hand in putting education back together in fresh, powerful, and more equitable ways that inspired generations of radical dreamers.

Our Stories: How We Came to This Work

Although it is hard for us to imagine a time when we didn't know each other, we started our lives as teachers in two different places at two different times and went on to teach in two very different schools. Despite all of these differences, both of our teaching careers were grounded in the practice of watching kids in order to let them take the lead in our instructional decision-making. We both recall hours spent in nursery school classrooms taking detailed notes on the moves and talk of children as they engaged in the messy work of learning through play. We were taught the value of sitting back to kidwatch as a way to honor and understand the ability of students to construct their own meanings, to solve their own problems, and to take charge of their learning.

Later in our work as classroom teachers in New York City public schools, we both had the opportunity to work alongside administrators, colleagues, and children who trusted us to make instructional decisions. We adjusted the timing of lessons as needed, picked read-alouds that matched the interests of our students, and made independent reading the centerpiece of our classrooms. We were trusted to watch our students closely and, after reflecting on our new understandings, put our expertise to work to make decisions. We were inspired to write this book because we were both fortunate enough to start our careers as teachers in supportive, trusting environments. We believe that all teachers and students today deserve to have that experience.

Some years ago, we were visiting a third-grade classroom in which the students were reading informational articles in partnerships. We noticed one student, head bent over a scrap of paper, drawing, while his partner seemed to be doing the actual reading. "Oh no," we thought, "what's going on over there?" We stood near the boys, careful not to interrupt right away. One partner was reading the article aloud, methodically working his way through the description of a sea turtle. The other partner was carefully sketching a sea turtle, using his partner's reading to guide to his work. Noticing us, he looked up and said, "We needed to visualize it." These boys helped us to remember the surprises kids have in store for us when we take time to let them show us who they are as readers.

Since leaving our own classrooms, both of us have noticed that despite exemplary teachers and a wealth of research in best practices, reading instruction has gone awry in many school communities. We began to ask ourselves what was getting in the way. After listening to administrators, teachers, and students, we came to realize that there is a crisis of trust around the teaching of reading. From a lack of investment in texts, to scripted curriculum, to rigid schedules, to too many mandated assessments—all of these problematic classroom realities were the result of a lack of trust.

Specifically, due to this crisis of trust, independent reading is too often viewed as a luxury rather than a right of every student. Instruction is no longer grounded in kidwatching, nor does it allow spaces for students to develop a sense of agency as readers. This instruction does not provide space for children or teachers to facilitate powerful learning experiences that allow children to construct their own meanings. Under these circumstances, it is difficult for teachers to trust themselves, their students, or that independent reading is enough, and this leads to reductionist instruction that prioritizes the delivery of skills and strategies over the development of a robust reading life or agentive class. When we trust ourselves as experts in our students and in the process of reading, we can make an impact. When we trust our students to be agentive partners, we can create reading experiences that impact students' growth and identity as readers.

How This Book Is Organized

In Part One, we define *independent reading* as based on the principles of time, choice, talk, and teacher support. We invite you to consider new spaces of possibility in order for vibrant independent reading to thrive in your classroom in visible and invisible ways.

In Part Two, we focus on the *reading conference*, inviting you to imagine new spaces of possibility for how to support your students to grow into being agentive, purposeful, engaged readers. We explore the Cycle of Conferring: the Discovery Conference, the Intention Conference, and the Impact Conference.

Throughout the book, you'll be directed to resources housed in our online resource collection. There you'll also find tips for supporting independent reading while teaching remotely (Online Resource I.1, Tips for Remote Learning).

We invite you to trust yourself to make decisions about what is best for the students in your classroom based on what you know about them. We invite you to trust your students to lead the way. We invite you to trust the beauty of naming students' strengths and using those as a jumping-off point. We invite you to trust in the power of having your own reading life. We invite you to trust that independent reading is the best way to move your students forward as readers.

Part One

Trust Independent Reading

"Social imagination is the capacity to invent visions of what should be and might be . . . in our schools."

—Maxine Greene

What's Happening to Independent Reading?

The wide benefits of voluminous independent reading are well established. Independent reading develops background knowledge and comprehension while improving motivation and reading achievement (Miller and Moss 2013). Students who read more score better on achievement tests (Calkins 2001). Reading volume, which is defined as time spent reading plus the number of words read, plays a key role in the development of reading proficiency (Allington 2012). Vibrant independent reading has also been linked to a better acquisition of skills, superior grades, and desirable life outcomes such as greater income levels and professional choices (Perie, Grigg, and Donahue 2005). Independent reading has been linked to developing more empathetic and emotionally resilient children (Routman 2002). Any way you look at it, independent reading has proven to be an indispensable and indisputable foundation for solid reading instruction. Yet, in many classrooms across the country, independent reading feels like a luxury rather than a central piece of the instructional school day. Why are so many teachers still finding it necessary to argue for protected time to provide this essential opportunity to their students? What is getting in the way of trusting the power of independent reading?

In a recent report, Scholastic (2019) found that 94 percent of teachers and principals believe that students should have more time to read a book of their choice during the school day, yet the average elementary school allocates only twenty-two minutes (or less) for independent reading. In the same survey, teachers who are in favor of increased time for independent reading share that the number one obstacle to this ideal is the time curriculum demands. When more emphasis is placed on fidelity to a curriculum than fidelity to the needs of students, teachers are operating within rigid time constraints, which robs them of the ability to provide time for independent reading and the flexibility necessary to be responsive to students. We believe that the time allocated to different learning opportunities reflects the value a school places on each opportunity. When time for independent reading is not protected, a greater value is being placed on mastery of curriculum than on developing vibrant independent reading lives.

The Role of Implicit Bias

A discussion of independent reading and getting to know our students as readers would be incomplete without acknowledging the role implicit bias plays in all aspects of our teaching. *Implicit bias* refers to the attitudes or stereotypes that affect our understanding, actions, and decisions in an unconscious manner. Implicit bias is activated involuntarily, without awareness or intentional control and can be either positive or negative. Everyone is susceptible (Staats et al. 2017). As educators positioned within a historically biased system, we have a responsibility to acknowledge our own biases and how they impact us as we listen to children talk about their identities as readers. This can be uncomfortable work, yet it is vital to our practice. Bias can manifest itself in the ways we view students and their potential. In her research, Gholdy Muhammad (2020) finds that deficit-oriented perspectives lead to poor and basic instructional practices. By acknowledging our implicit bias and working to be aware of the way it can influence our interactions with students and aiming to change those interactions and decisions that further inequities, we increase our ability to approach all students knowing there are a variety of ways to value reading and incorporate reading into their lives.

Independent Reading Redefined

Historically, independent reading has taken a variety of forms and, therefore, looks different in different schools (Miller and Moss 2013). The acronyms to represent variations of reading time are like an alphabet soup: we have SSR (sustained silent reading), DEAR (drop everything and read), SQUIRT (sustained quiet uninterrupted reading time), and FVR (free voluntary reading), just to name a few. But what do these all really mean? In all these letters, how can we piece together a clear vision? Also muddled in the midst of this alphabet soup is a clear vision of the roles of both student and teacher.

What might it look like when trusting relationships honor the expertise and stories of students and teachers? In 2019, the National Council of Teachers of English (NCTE) published a position statement that defined *independent reading* as routine, protected instructional practice that includes time for students to read, receive support within a reading community, and have access to books. It named student choice as essential to independent reading because it motivates and engages a wide variety of readers. NCTE went on to state that a primary goal of independent reading is to build habitual readers with clear reading identities. The International Literacy Association's Children's Rights to Read movement (2020), outlined ten rights children possess with regard to access and time in reading. These rights echo the position of NCTE on independent reading, maintaining that time, choice, access to text, expert support, and opportunity to share ideas are critical rights of students.

Independent reading honors these well-researched stances and creates spaces for students and teachers to engage with text in ways that encourage students to actively construct their own meanings and ask their own questions.

Building on this vision, our definition of impactful independent reading is based on four principles: time, choice, talk, and teacher support.

Time + Choice + Talk + Teacher Support = Impactful Independent Reading

1. **Time:** Students need and deserve long stretches of time to lose themselves and find themselves in books. There is a direct correlation between increased reading skills and the amount of time engaged in reading (Allington and Gabriel 2012). During this time, students transfer previously taught skills and strategies into independence as they make meaning from text. When students have ample time to read, they build the capacity to engage and reengage, building authentic stamina.

   Teachers need and deserve long stretches of time to kidwatch and admire students' strengths as readers. Teachers use these long stretches of time to support student growth by providing feedback to each student. When teachers value independent reading, they prioritize time for it every day.

2. **Choice:** Students are more motivated to read and engage with complex text when they choose texts themselves (Allington and Gabriel 2012). With choice, students have the space to explore, construct, and expand their identities as readers. As teachers and schools build classroom libraries for children to choose from, it is important to include texts that represent a diverse range of experiences and identities. To do this requires an examination of biases that may unconsciously get in the way of making certain that all students have access to books—both in which they can find themselves and in which they are given opportunities to develop empathy for others.

3. **Talk:** In order to expand and deepen their ability to make meaning from text, students need to have regular opportunities to talk with their teachers and peers in a variety of forms. Not only does talk boost engagement, but it aids in the development of social comprehension as students learn to listen, to imagine, and to empathize with both characters and, ultimately, classmates.

   In order to feel confident in taking risks, students need to trust and expect their teacher will strive to see their entire selves, honor their reading identities, and make them feel cared for as they support their growth as readers. As students' opportunities for talk increase, teachers gain the opportunity to do more listening. Teachers listen to student talk to understand the ways in which their students contribute to collective meaning-making experiences. Teachers also listen to understand various aspects of students' reading identities and, at the same time, uncover the stories of students' whole selves.

4. **Teacher support:** We want to be absolutely clear. Simply giving students time to read is not the same as independent reading. Supporting robust independent reading includes nurturing student reading identities, growing stamina, teaching targeted skills and strategies, establishing partnerships, and boosting students' trust in themselves. Joyful independent reading does not happen by accident; it is a conscious collaboration between teachers and students.

The Role of Trust in Independent Reading

In psychology, *trust* is defined as believing that the person who is trusted will do what is expected. The American Psychological Association's *APA Dictionary of Psychology* (2020) states that trust is considered to be a primary component in all mature relationships regardless of the context. In business, trust is defined as holding people accountable without micromanaging them. "You cultivate trust by setting a clear direction, giving people what they need to see it through, and getting out of their way" (Zak 2017).

In schools specifically, cultivating trust means that administrators are expected to create a vision for the school and to support teachers to carry out that vision. Teachers are expected to engage the whole child every day. Students should be able to bring their whole selves to their work in the classroom. When teachers, administrators, and students trust each other to do what is expected, everyone thrives. When trust abounds, administrators have confidence in teachers to make wise decisions. Teachers have confidence in themselves to provide the right teaching at the right time for all students. Students trust their peers and feel at home in the classroom. Students have confidence in themselves as learners. Trust allows both teachers and students to take risks as learners and revel in developing vibrant reading lives.

Trusting Readers: Powerful Practices for Independent Reading

We trust that students enter our classrooms already living their reading lives. Prior to entering school, students have had opportunities to interact with and make meaning from a variety of texts including oral storytelling, videos, or songs in addition to possibly being read to or reading texts themselves. Our work is to honor and nurture these reading identities by making space for students to continue to grow and expand upon the types of meaning making that fuel their desire to read.

Specifically, we trust that students already have their own purposes for reading, their own reading preferences, and their own authentic ways to respond to text. We trust that these strengths are the best starting points for instruction. We trust that readers can lead our instruction.

We trust that all students are readers.

Trusting Teachers

We trust that teachers are reflective practitioners open to feedback from students as well as their peers. We trust that teachers have the capacity to be agentive, engaged learners alongside their students. We trust the expertise of teachers and their ability to direct their own professional development, seeking out learning communities and recent research that both supports and deepens their thinking about the teaching of reading. We trust the power of teachers having authentic reading lives, including reading lots of children's literature. We trust teachers to celebrate and share their successes.

We trust that in the classroom teachers possess an asset-minded stance toward students by creating instructional opportunities based on students' strengths. We trust that teachers value and engage in regular kidwatching to inform instructional decision-making. We trust that teachers are responsible for and capable of acknowledging their own biases and how these biases influence their understandings of children and their experiences.

We trust teachers to teach readers.

A Call to Action: Why the Urgency for Independent Reading Now?

Equity minded educators understand that education requires high expectations for all students.

—Sheldon Eakins

If we want our students to be active participants in their own reading education, we need to model this sense of agency for them by building in time to read with targeted teacher support. When we allow the schedule to dictate how we spend our time, we are not showing students how to be agents in their own learning. When we leave reading time out, we are perhaps unconsciously making harmful assumptions about students' equitable access to texts outside of school. In this age of accountability, being agentive teachers and cultivating agentive readers is a radical act that pushes back against standardization.

A seminal study conducted by the Annie E. Casey Foundation (Hernandez 2012) shows that reaching reading proficiency by third grade is a clear predictor of academic success. And yet Scholastic's *Kids and Family Reading Report* (2019) finds that third-grade children's frequency of reading books for fun begins to drop; only 35 percent of nine-year-olds report reading five to seven days a week, compared with 57 percent of eight-year-olds. Further, despite statistics that link reading proficiency to future success in school, there is overwhelming evidence that it is specifically children in lower-income communities who tend to have far less access to texts than children in higher-income communities (Krashen 2004). Independent reading should not be a luxury for any child. Educational equity demands that we do what we know works best for all students rather than some students. Independent reading is every student's right.

A Moment for Reflection

We invite teachers to flip the question from "What should I do?" to "What does the research suggest and what do my students need me to do?" When we place more trust in teachers, we empower them to define and grow their own practice in response to the evolving needs and interests of students.

Take a moment to reflect on your current reading practice and the place of independent reading in your classroom. Reconsider the following core principles of independent reading as a way to reflect.

Principles of Independent Reading

Principle	What is it?	Why?	How?
Time	• Students need 30 minutes a day to read. • In the younger grades, build up stamina over time. • Reading can occur at different times of day as students build stamina.	• Volume of reading is key to growth. • Students need time to read in volume.	• Start by including 30–60 minutes in your schedule for students to read. • Add in 15 minutes for whole-group instruction. • Even if your students are not yet reading for that amount of time, the time is protected. • Prioritize independent reading when planning by putting it into your plans first, not last. • Celebrate where students already are in their stamina and build from that point.

continues

Principle	What is it?	Why?	How?
Choice	• The classroom library is well stocked and managed by the students. • Students read a variety of books: some books are on students' independent level; some are of high interest to the students.	• Students are more motivated to read and engaged in their reading when they get to choose what they read. • Engagement is necessary for deep learning to occur.	• Students have access to all the books in the library. • Support students in choosing books that both honor and stretch their reading identities. • Conduct class discussions about considerations when choosing books. • Advertise books and invite students to advertise books.
Talk	• Talk occurs during student partnerships, book clubs, book talks, and regular opportunities to share.	• Talk leads to improved comprehension and empathy and builds community.	• Include partner time in independent reading. • Conduct inquiries into purposeful talk. • Confer with partners and clubs about talk. • Read aloud throughout the day to encourage talk.
Teacher support	• Teacher support can come in a variety of forms: whole-class lessons, conferences, and small-group lessons. • Teacher support builds upon established student strengths.	• Feedback is one of the most impactful tools we have for raising student achievement.	• Analyze big and small data to imagine next steps. • Design a schedule that includes conferring and small-group work. • Take notes during conferences and small-group work. • Be prepared to teach.

As you move through this book, keep these principles in mind. We invite you to imagine new spaces of possibility for yourself and for your students. What is the best that could happen if you trusted yourself, your students, and the power of independent reading?

1

All Roads Lead to Independent Reading

Independent reading is far from the entire reading curriculum, but what children do during independent reading should affect, and be affected by, the entire curriculum. Too often in the teaching of reading, the separate components of the reading curriculum exist independently of each other.

—Lucy Calkins

Imagine this: You are visiting a first-grade classroom during independent reading. Children are scattered throughout the room, some curled up on their own, some reading alongside partners. A few children are talking quietly to one another; others are reading silently. The teacher is not easy to spot at first; they are sitting alongside a reader, their heads bent over a book. Your eye is drawn to the library as one child walks over and offers their book to another student who is looking for something to read. The many baskets of books all have labels created by students. Some are predictable—"Books About Animals" or "Stories About School"—while others are less so, such as "Books That Make You Laugh" or "Scary Books About Animal Attacks." There are displays of books around topics the class has studied: realistic fiction, cultural traditions around the world, and winter. When you walk over to a child and ask what they are doing as a reader, the child says, "I'm working on

retelling the stories I read from beginning to end to see which ones have a happy ending. I want to make a new basket for our classroom library."

This classroom is built on trust; students are clearly trusted to be in charge of their reading lives. The teacher trusts that when they give students time and choice, students are more likely to become engaged in their reading. The students trust their teacher to support and guide them, and they take her feedback seriously. The students trust each other to recommend books, to understand one another as readers, and to share their learning with one another. By relying on the principles of time, choice, talk, and teacher support, the teacher trusts that these children will grow as readers who will be able to make meaning from increasingly complex and varied texts.

In this chapter, we address how all of the parts of the literacy block, punctuated with invitations for engagement and talk, weave together to lead students to read independently. If you are using a balanced literacy approach, this means that all the components of balanced literacy tie together in support of independent reading. If you are teaching using a different model, you can still prioritize independent reading time, creating connections between all reading experiences across the day. Regardless, we invite you to flip the question from "How can I fit it all in?" to "How are all of the parts of the literacy block and all of my teaching methods working together?"

Crafting Instruction That Inspires Independent Reading

Each day, teachers have the opportunity to craft relevant learning experiences that inspire their particular group of students. This privilege requires that we trust ourselves as experts in our field as well as experts in our students to make decisions that contribute to joyful, agentive, routine independent reading. Teaching has the potential to be a radical act if teachers act with agency themselves by seeking out spaces of possibility within the school day and imagining what ought to be, rather than simply accepting what is (Greene 1995). When daily literacy opportunities are crafted with the goal of creating independent readers, rather than delivering instruction related to a list of skills and strategies, instructional decision-making originates with students themselves at the center. In addition, the collective reading experiences throughout the school day hold the potential to build the foundation of trust needed as students work together to take risks and construct meaning from complex texts both together and independently.

Independent Reading

Read Aloud

Shared Reading

Small-Group Instruction

Word Study

Curriculum

Each day, students need the opportunity to engage in relevant learning experiences. Students need equitable access to research-backed structures and practices, such as independent reading and read-aloud, that are proven to contribute to their growth as readers and thinkers (International Literacy Association 2018). One way to create equitable instruction is to work to understand the story of each student so that you can tailor learning opportunities to build upon and be relevant to their strengths and experiences.

All the components of robust literacy instruction work together to create relevant instruction. The structure of the school day sometimes forces us to divide our time into blocks. Each component on its own can be both joyful and impactful, yet no one component can stand completely on its own. While *we* are clear about the purpose of each block, our students may see them as unrelated to each other and to their independent reading unless we clearly communicate the ways in which all parts of the literacy block work together in the service of independent reading.

In planning these individual components with the needs of independent readers in mind, consider these guiding questions:

- How do these learning experiences honor and respond to the identities of all my students?

  ○ How does each part of my instruction today grow the skills, knowledge, and identities of independent readers?

  ○ What are the strengths of my students? How can I highlight and build upon those strengths during instruction?

  ○ What are the next steps for my students? How can I model or facilitate practice with these next steps?

See the chart on page 12 for some sample responses to these questions.

A Balanced Literacy Perspective

Balanced literacy has been interpreted to mean the balance between direct and dialogic instruction, the balance between whole-group, small-group, and individual instruction, the balance between phonics and authentic reading, and the balance between reading and writing (Fisher, Fry, and Akhavan 2019). While the term can encompass all of these definitions, at its core, it is an approach that supports the development of independent readers and writers through a variety of teaching components. We refer here specifically to the components of literacy instruction: read-aloud, shared reading, small-group reading instruction, phonics and word study, and writing.

Typically, within a balanced literacy framework, teachers work within reading units of study. These units of study might be purchased from an outside resource or created in-house by teachers. In order to provide consistency, units of study fit within a pacing calendar that guides reading instruction across the year. Generally, some units are based on genre while others are based on process or skill.

In the following sections, we describe each component of balanced literacy, highlighting how each supports independent reading. Each component presents opportunities for explicit transfer talk. If you are teaching in a different framework or using a set curriculum, this section can help you think about multiple ways to support independent reading throughout the day, within your own context. Independent reading plays a vital role in every literacy curriculum and program. Trust yourself to plan so that all of your instruction is in the service of independent reading.

Tailoring Learning Experiences to Student Skills, Knowledge, and Identity	
Reflection Question	**Sample Response**
How does each part of my instruction today grow the skills, knowledge, and identities of independent readers?	*The skill we are working on is determining the main idea in informational text. I am teaching the strategy of reading a chunk of text and thinking, "What is this mostly about?"* *I plan to grow students' knowledge of our science unit of study on the water cycle by using one of our read-alouds to model this strategy.* *I know, through kidwatching, that most of my students prefer fiction, specifically graphic novels. I plan to use an informational text that uses similar features to connect to that aspect of their reading identity.*
What are the strengths of my students? How can I high-light those strengths during instruction?	*The data shows me that Yuko is a student who prefers informational text and is already doing this work with independence. I can ask her to share her thinking with the class in a text of her choosing.*
What are the next steps for my students? How can I model or facilitate practice with these next steps?	*The data shows me that a majority of my students need to practice with this strategy. After this lesson, I can determine if we are ready to incorporate the use of visual features to determine the main idea.* *I can have students work in partnerships to practice so I can listen in to their conversations. They can choose any informational book that interests them or use familiar informational read-alouds, select a section, and give this a go. I might have them write and post their thoughts on sticky notes.* *Students can then continue to read informational texts for the entirety of independent reading time, or they can decide to read other independent reading books.*

How Curriculum Can Support Independent Reading

Rigid or set curriculum is often cited as the number one roadblock to including more independent reading time in classrooms. Curriculum might feel irrelevant to the students in front of you, too filled with tasks and activities to allow space for independence. For teachers, curriculum might feel too time-consuming to cover. However, when we move to using relevant curriculum to *uncover* and build upon what our students already know, it can serve to expand the work of independent readers. It can offer new possibilities; it can inspire readers to try a new genre or strategy or grow their knowledge about the world around them.

Here's a typical scenario: when a class is immersed in a unit on informational texts, fiction-loving students who might be in the middle of an exciting series may acutely feel the lack of choice, and their engagement may decrease. By recognizing this, we can act purposefully to reframe the choices. For example, you might ask students to read informational text for the first few minutes of independent reading and then open up choice, or you could provide familiar engaging read-aloud texts as an option, or you might place students in interest-based partnerships. Flip the question from "How can I fit in the work of the unit and independent reading?" to "How can I bring this unit to life in ways that support independent readers?" New possibilities then come to mind. Units of study turn into a way of expanding reading identity. The chart on page 14 provides examples of how various units of study can be reframed to support independent reading and readers.

How the Read-Aloud Supports Independent Reading

The read-aloud provides limitless joyful possibilities for meaning making. When we open up the invitation for students to respond as we read a carefully chosen text, we find that students do not need us to prompt them; rather, they authentically respond to actively construct meaning from the text, just as they do while reading independently. Their eyes might widen, giggles might ripple across the rug, or, in particularly juicy moments, children might exclaim out loud.

As with independent reading, the research on the role of the read-aloud is vast. According to a recent International Literacy Association brief, "reading aloud is undoubtedly one of the most important instructional activities to help children

Curriculum and Independent Reading

Curriculum	How It Supports Independent Reading
Units at the beginning of the year focus on routines and expectations for the reading block.	These units provide space to explore reading identity and the classroom library.
Genre-based units of study introduce students to the genre and to related skills and strategies.	These expand reading identity and promote an opportunity to practice actively reflecting on book choice.
Process-based units of study introduce students to essential skills and strategies that apply across genres.	These add to a student's sense of self-efficacy, growing a list of what each reader can do.
Units that utilize book clubs encourage students to study a particular author, genre, theme, or identity.	These promote opportunities for specific instruction to support talk and how it can expand meaning making.

develop the fundamental skills and knowledge to become readers" (2018, 2). Research has shown read-alouds improve comprehension (Duke and Pearson 2009), vocabulary (Massaro 2017), and fluency (Trelease 2001). Further, the read-aloud is one of many opportunities to grow students' knowledge of the world around them, their social comprehension (Ahmed 2018), and their ability to be critical consumers of text.

The read-aloud is a key piece of literacy instruction, as it supports and inspires independent reading and response to reading in the classroom. The following are examples of read-aloud charts from first- and fourth-grade classrooms.

During the READ ALOUD, we can (TALK) about...

- new words

- favorite parts

- favorite characters

- What it makes us (think) about?

- How it makes us feel...

- What did we learn?
  What do we still wonder?

- What surprised us?

During the READ ALOUD, we can
(TALK) about...

- characters and their relationships
- characters and how they change

- What does the author want us to learn?

- What does it make us THINK about?
- How does it make us FEEL?
- How does it impact your BELIEFS?
- What does it make you want TO DO?

- What surprised you?
- What do you still wonder?

- What beautiful language stands out?

What is worth talking about?

The chart below captures some of the ways in which the read-aloud inspires the work of independent readers.

Read-Aloud and Independent Reading	
Read-Aloud	How It Supports Independent Reading
Teachers model aspects of the reading process including fluent reading and comprehension strategies.	Students read more expressively and apply those comprehension strategies to make meaning in their own texts.
Teachers read from a wide range of books and discuss book choice, using the read-aloud to get students excited about new topics, series, and authors.	Students reflect on and expand their book choices.
Teachers teach, model, and facilitate talk moves that lead to lively, authentic class discussions. This may include translanguaging.	Students can practice these talk moves in their discussions with partners and book clubs. This may include translanguaging, the practice of encouraging students to use their complete language repertoire to interact with text (España and Hererra 2020).
Teachers can select read-alouds to build a sense of community, tackle various obstacles that may arise across the year, and work to develop social comprehension.	Students can use the read-aloud as a place to think about and process common classroom issues or larger social issues that may also play out in the classroom. Students can then bring this thinking work into their independent reading. In this way, independent reading can become a vehicle for learning about the lives and experiences of others.
Teachers direct attention to new vocabulary and how readers might determine the meaning of and utilize newly acquired words.	Students grow their vocabulary and background knowledge to support their comprehension in various content areas.

How Shared Reading Supports Independent Reading

In shared reading, teachers and students have access to a common, engaging text that provides opportunities for the students to expand their use of skills and strategies (Parks 1999). In kindergarten through second grade, teachers might use big books, classroom charts, songs, and poems. In grades three through five, teachers can use materials such as a few paragraphs from a read-aloud, a short article, a poem, or song lyrics. Together, teachers and students work from this shared text multiple times during the week, highlighting a new way for making meaning each time. There is a natural overlap between shared reading and the read-aloud, but a key difference is that in shared reading, the students are doing the work of looking at the print and punctuation, reading the words with the teacher. Not only does shared reading give all students appropriate access to complex, grade-level texts, but it gives students another scaffolded opportunity to engage with print in ways that support their specific needs as readers.

For a thorough discussion of shared reading, refer to *The Fountas and Pinnell Literacy Continuum* (Fountas and Pinnell 2017) and Brenda Parks' *Read It Again!* (1999).

The following chart captures the ways in which the work of shared reading can support and inspire the work of independent readers.

Shared Reading and Independent Reading	
Shared Reading	**How It Supports Independent Reading**
Shared reading focuses first on enjoyment and comprehension while also exposing students to a variety of genres and topics.	Students expect independent reading to feel joyful. They welcome the opportunity to try new genres and topics.
Shared reading models the act of rereading a text with a specific purpose while also making grade-level texts more familiar and accessible to all students.	Students read and reread their independent books as well as copies of the shared text, trying on a variety of purposes and lenses.
Shared reading allows teachers to model multiple skills and strategies for word solving and fluency.	Students can apply the same skills and strategies when working independently to solve words in their texts.
Shared reading provides the whole class, small groups, or partnerships another opportunity to construct meaning together.	Students may transfer new ways to make meaning from text to their independent reading work.

How Small-Group Instruction Supports Independent Reading

Small-group instruction allows teachers to tailor instruction to match student needs. It is a highly flexible and responsive structure that can take many forms. Although small-group instruction in reading typically refers to guided reading and strategy groups, any whole-class component can also be used with a small group. *Guided reading* is a structure in which teachers gather together students at a similar instructional level to support them through the reading of an appropriate, unfamiliar text (Fountas and Pinnell 2017). As teachers listen to and coach students through reading the text, opportunities for teaching points emerge. A *strategy group* involves a group of students with the same instructional need (Serravallo 2015). Children read their independent reading books, working to apply the strategy.

Small-group instruction originates with the question "What patterns am I observing?" and moves to "What is the most effective way to teach into that pattern?" We can imagine a wealth of possibilities for small groups that include but also reach beyond grouping students by instructional reading levels. The chart below captures some of the ways in which small-group instruction can support independent reading.

Small-Group Reading Instruction and Independent Reading	
Type of Small Group	**How It Supports Independent Reading**
Guided reading supports students as they read at their instructional level. Teachers carefully pick the text and respond to students' reading by prompting, reinforcing, and teaching.	Students expand the range of text at which they feel comfortable reading with independence, utilizing strategies for reading increasingly complex texts.
Strategy groups support students with direct instruction in specific strategies that represent targeted opportunities for growth.	Students call upon this work while reading, transferring these strategies into independence.
Shared reading in a small group is a highly scaffolded support for students who are focusing on fluency and word solving.	These students add shared reading texts to their independent reading selections, which can expand the variety of reading they can do independently.
Using interactive read-aloud in a small group supports students in making meaning from text as well as developing strategies for talking about books.	These students add read-aloud texts to their independent reading selections. With the additional time to practice talking in a small group, students gain confidence to initiate and contribute to conversations when working with a partner.

How Phonics, Word Work, and Spelling Support Independent Reading

A print-rich environment that includes systematic phonics instruction is critical to the success of independent readers. Research is clear that students need to acquire phonics and word analysis understandings and that they need to apply these understandings to reading and writing (Fountas and Pinnell 2017). This includes phonological awareness, letter knowledge, letter-sound relationships, spelling, and vocabulary. This sort of word study does not thrive in isolation; rather, it is an essential component to instruction that serves the development of independent readers and writers in clear ways.

Proficient, fluent readers are able to call upon phonological knowledge to solve words. Once students are able to efficiently solve words, they are more able to turn their attention to advancing their comprehension work. As illustrated below, the integration and transfer of regular phonics instruction needs to be in the service of and in response to the work of independent readers.

Phonics and Independent Reading	
Explicit Phonics Instruction	**How It Supports Independent Reading**
Students develop phonological awareness.	With direct transfer support, students integrate their phonics instruction into their independent reading work, helping them to crack the code and read texts fully and with independence.
Students gain alphabetic knowledge.	
Students gain exposure to and practice with decoding and encoding a bank of sight words.	
Students accumulate specific word-solving strategies.	

How Writing Workshop Supports Independent Reading

Regardless of how you teach writing, reading and writing relate to one another in a myriad of ways. We can assume that working effectively in one activity will help with work in the other (Clay 2005). Both readers and writers enter their work with a purpose, monitor for meaning, infer, and envision. Reading and writing both help students connect to the world and feel known. Both are about meaning making: reading is the message getting, and writing is the message sending. A student's proficiency as a reader and as a writer often grows hand in hand. As we make the connections between these two acts more concrete for children, both reading and writing can serve as supports for one another.

The following chart illustrates a few of the many ways in which reading and writing connect.

Writing Workshop and Independent Reading	
Writing Workshop	**How It Supports Independent Reading**
Writers understand that their writing conveys meaning.	Readers consider the author's purpose for writing and how it impacts the meaning they make from the text.
Writers compose in a variety of genres and understand how the genres work.	Readers transfer what they learn from writing in a new genre to help them be better able to make meaning in that genre.
Writers choose their words and phrases with care.	Readers pay attention to authors' word choices in order to glean greater meaning from the text and expand their own vocabularies.
Writers intentionally use punctuation to guide the reader.	Readers pay attention to punctuation to read fluently and to consider how punctuation influences meaning making.

Talk and Independent Reading

When our own children were younger, we would get nervous when they were too quiet. Were they doing something mischievous? Sneaking cookies from the kitchen? Playing with slime on the furniture? Similarly, we get nervous when classrooms are too quiet during independent reading.

Learning is a relational act that relies upon trusting relationships, shared learning experiences, and the active participation of students. Talk both requires and builds trust. When teachers rely on dialogic teaching methods, talk flows *between* teachers and students—all class members work collaboratively to grow shared understandings as they tackle critical questions for inquiry. Classrooms alive with purposeful talk convey a shared understanding that our thinking grows stronger together.

When students are engaged in their reading, the classroom may be buzzing as opposed to silent. Readers lean over to share gross parts of their nonfiction books, exclaim over a plot twist, or ask for help with a word. Purposeful talk indicates high levels of engagement, allows students to develop their thinking, and allows us to glimpse that thinking. Understandably, we hope for high-quality talk during independent reading; we may wonder if the students are really talking about their books or if they are talking about what's for lunch. But when we devote time to teaching into talk—both into kinds of talk and purposes for talk—and when we trust that students will stick to talking about their books *most* of the time, they will get more out of reading and will sustain reading for longer.

How Talk Supports Independent Reading

Here are some ways that talk supports independent reading:

1. **Talk builds relationships.** As students engage in purposeful talk around reading, they begin to reveal their identities as readers, forming connections that may stretch beyond other social connections. For example, they might find new friendships with others who share similar preferences or come to understand one another's experiences differently as they connect over a shared text.

2. **Talk develops ideas.** As students engage in purposeful talk with constructive intent (Nichols 2019), they play with and expand upon nascent ideas. With guidance, students may engage in purposeful talk to clarify, analyze, and argue their ideas about text with others and, in this way, revise their own ideas accordingly.

3. **Talk shares and grows perspectives.** Talk allows students to contribute their ideas to the larger group to extend meaning making. As each child explains how they construct meaning from a given text, the meaning-making ability of the entire class grows and deepens as they consider the varied perspectives of their peers. When we allow time for conversations to develop, the collective meaning making grows more relevant and impactful.

Along with talk comes listening. Purposeful talk requires that students share their ideas clearly and then revise or strengthen these ideas by closely listening to the perspectives of others (Frazin and Wischow 2020). The purposes of listening closely mirror the purposes of talk. Here are some ways that listening supports independent reading:

1. **Listening builds and strengthens relationships.** As students listen to their peers talk about their reading and reveal pieces of their identities as readers, the potential for new connection points grows exponentially. Children are able to see more complete pictures of one another, creating spaces for more empathetic relationships. Further, students are then able to think more deeply about their own identity as it relates to others.

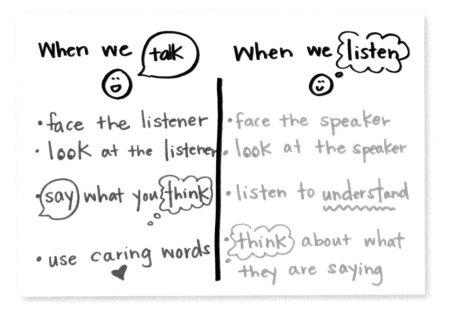

When we (talk)
• face the listener
• look at the listener
• (say) what you {think}
• use caring words

When we {listen}
• face the speaker
• look at the speaker
• listen to understand
• {think} about what they are saying

2. **Listening provides information.** When students listen as their peers construct meaning from text, they begin to accumulate varied perspectives and adapt their own accordingly. Being exposed to a variety of perspectives not only develops empathy for others but also solidifies the notion that there is no single meaning we should take from text.

3. **Listening changes or grows thinking.** When students listen to process the perspectives of their peers, they develop empathy while also extending their own ability to make meaning. In addition, students may experience an engaged sense of perspective bending (Keene 2018) as their thinking about text and the world begins to grow and shift in response to the thinking of others.

The above chart created by a first-grade class is about talking and listening.

How Partnerships Support Independent Reading

Although partnerships tend to be emphasized in the lower grades, we find that partnerships nurture independent reading engagement and deepen meaning making at all grade levels. Routinely scheduling time for partners to meet and discuss their reading is one way to encourage talk, and it also creates opportunities for teachers to kidwatch or teach into specific talk (and listening) moves. Partnerships are most effective when they are flexible and change throughout the year. This serves to encourage talk across students who may not otherwise seek each other out and, over time, strengthens trust within the classroom community.

Not only is partnering students in a variety of ways a more equitable decision, but it also opens up new possibilities for students' reading identity, relationships, meaning making, and talk. Regularly partnering students by a benchmarked level can turn into de facto ability grouping, which fails to benefit any student. Beyond levels, if we always partner students in the same way, we run the risk of inadvertently cementing an aspect of their reading identity, thus creating an obstacle for growth. In addition, consider the potential for engagement when students form their own partnerships based on commonalities that speak to who they are as readers in the moment. Imagine the possibilities that are created when partnering students in the following ways.

Varied Partnerships, Varied Talk		
Ways to Partner Students	**What It Means and How to Do It**	**How It Inspires Talk**
By habits	Match students who read in similar ways or spaces, such as those who like to read under desks or sneak in reading throughout the day.	In sharing how and where they like to read, partners can begin to grow ideas about their varied purposes for reading.
By interests	Match students who enjoy reading similar authors, around similar themes or topics, or within a similar genre.	In talking about their book preferences, partners can deepen their understanding of how a series works, grow their knowledge around a shared topic of interest, or inspire additional book choices by a related author.

continues

Ways to Partner Students	What It Means and How to Do It	How It Inspires Talk
By process	Match students who share a similar strength or those who have similar goals. Both pairings can lead to deep work and encourage talk around a particular aspect of comprehension.	In reflecting on and sharing their process with one another, partners can grow their repertoire and encourage the transfer of taught skills and strategies into independent reading.
By choice	Students create their own partnerships based on their affinities.	In self-selecting partners, students may feel a greater comfort level with one another, which can lead to more constructive and joyful talk.

Engagement and Independent Reading

When your students groan at the end of reading time and insist on carrying their books with them to recess, you know that they are engaged in their reading. Engagement is "the infectious enthusiasm students display when working on something of personal interest pursued inductively" (Renzulli 2008). Engagement in learning is one of the major contributors to student achievement (Fisher, Frey, and Quaglia 2018). Trust plays a key role in this work, as trusting relationships between students and teachers are the foundation of thriving classrooms that intentionally invite engagement in reading (Purkey and Novak 1996). When shared trust exists, students are more likely to take risks.

If you would like to delve more deeply into engagement, we highly recommend Ellin Oliver Keene's *Engaging Children: Igniting a Drive for Deeper Learning, K–8* (2018).

Despite the research, engagement can often seem like an abstract idea. When we refer to engagement, we mean that feeling that comes over us when we are truly engrossed and invested in an experience. Take a moment and think about a time when you were truly *engaged* in something—when you lost track of time in the most wonderful way and came out on the other side with new understandings about yourself or the world or perhaps with a solution to a complex problem.

Children possess a visceral understanding of what it means to be engaged. When we ask children to describe a time when they felt engrossed, they share stories that take place in the kitchen, on the soccer field, or on playdates. Children can also tell us specific moments when they have been disengaged, bored, or overwhelmed. We do not expect students to be engaged every minute of the day. Neither are we. Our job is to understand what our students find engaging and to create *the conditions for engagement* in our classrooms.

Our vision is that all our students will experience engagement in their reading. When students are engaged in their reading, they are transferring their learning into independence in order to make meaning from text. Inviting students to become engaged readers is not about using jazz hands and being entertaining (although we do generally appreciate a good use of jazz hands whenever possible). It is about talking with students to name the feeling of engagement and setting up the conditions for students to become engaged in reading in authentic ways. It is about opening up inquiries into and conversations about what it means to be engaged, how to get reengaged, and what we find engaging.

In addition to a foundation of trust, classrooms that "intentionally invite" (Fisher, Frey, and Quaglia 2018, 6) engagement during independent reading share a few more visible factors:

> When I am engaged in reading...
>
> I can't wait to do it.
> I don't want to stop.
> I'm in my imagination.
> I feel hypnotized.
> I take the book to recess.
> I miss the bus.
> I'm in the book.

- Teachers conduct ongoing conversations about engagement itself, encouraging students to be aware of their own levels of engagement.

- Teachers encourage and teach children to monitor and adjust their own levels of engagement.

- Teachers provide multiple rich talk opportunities: talk between partners, talk with the teacher, and talk with the larger group.

- The physical environment reflects a sense of shared ownership and a love of reading in observable ways, including cocreated anchor charts, student-made charts, and an extensive and inclusive library.

Growing Students' Energy in Reading: Reimagining Stamina

Research emphasizes the benefits of reading in volume (Allington 2013). To encourage students to read for longer stretches of time, teachers often use timers, graph the minutes daily and monthly, require students to log numbers of pages, and cheer on students to read for "just five more minutes." These well-intended practices inadvertently narrow the definition of stamina. When the word *stamina* is synonymous with the number of minutes a child or a class is able to read, the emphasis is on time alone. It positions reading as something that children must grit their teeth and bear, as if stamina were similar to endurance. We worry that this definition of stamina is counterproductive and leads to compliance, fake reading, and students dreading reading time. When students are authentically engaged in their reading, stamina is something that grows naturally in the classroom, as opposed to something we need to push.

We propose a reimagined definition of stamina that is synonymous with reading engagement and joy. By viewing stamina as a by-product of deep engagement (Dinnerstein 2016), we are able to focus our teaching on reading as meaning making. As a result, children will naturally begin to read for longer and longer stretches. When we use the lens of engagement to think about stamina, we are better able to incorporate joy and agency as central to the work of reading independently for longer periods of time. Questions such as "How can I stay engaged as a reader?" "How can I pick books that keep me engaged?" and "What do I want to do as a reader tomorrow?" move to the forefront of stamina instruction. Time, in this view, becomes a concrete way to measure this growth over time and not the main goal.

We can keep reading by...

- ..."staying engaged" (Grace)
- ..."trying strategies on our own"... (Juan)
- ..."knowing WHY we are reading today" (Aiysha)
- ..."choosing books we are excited about"... (Lily)
- ..."finding a good-for-me reading spot"... (Jamar)

Trust Your Teaching

In keeping with our vision that all literacy instruction leads to independent reading, we rely on transfer to tie it all together. When we start with strengths as a jumping-off point to determine next steps for students, we are able to purposefully select the teaching structures that support the transference of feedback into independence. The more we do this, the more confidence we'll have to build literacy schedules that serve the needs of readers first.

Hold on to your vision of what literacy instruction ought to be and can be for your students. As we position ourselves as problem solvers and meaning makers alongside our students, it becomes our joyful duty to problematize and adjust instruction so that it serves to promote the growth of independent reading. We must trust ourselves as decision makers and we must trust the power of the engaged reader.

2

Trust the Classroom

The classroom environment, including the library, your routines, what you put on the walls, serves as a third teacher. Teachers observe the children in these possibility-rich environments, and on the basis of shared observations and documentations, they construct new possibilities for the children.

—Leila Gandini

In a fifth-grade classroom last spring, we were kidwatching while the students read independently. Anastasia was finishing her book. We watched her close it with a satisfying thud and then look around. We wondered what she might do next, interested to learn more about her habits as a reader. After a few minutes, Anastasia made her way to the library. We knew already that she was an avid Jason Reynolds fan, but that basket in the library was currently empty. She stood for a moment, looking at the baskets available, and then moved to look closely at a chart of book stacks on display nearby. Each student had curated a stack of books they wanted to recommend to others in the classroom; Anastasia scanned it, studying the list of one student in particular, and then went about finding one of the books suggested.

Later, when we talked to Anastasia, she said she had looked carefully at the book stack recommended by one classmate in particular because she knew they had a similar

taste in books. Using anchor charts and the collectively organized system of the classroom library, Anastasia stayed engaged as a reader and was able to independently navigate selecting a new book with no disruption to the class or the teacher.

Trusting the classroom to act as a third teacher means that the classroom environment is responsive to the needs of both teachers and students. Strategic classroom design can inspire engagement, independence, and academic risk-taking, conveying to students that this is a space in which we build new understandings together.

How Inclusive Classroom Libraries Support Independent Reading

Imagine a world in which all children can see themselves in the pages of a book.

—We Need Diverse Books website

The location and design of the classroom library send a clear message: "All readers are valued here." Although there are endless possibilities for how to organize the library, there are some key considerations. The ideal classroom library is organized to inspire readers, is accessible, and encourages students to use it independently. It includes texts that represent diverse perspectives, identities, as well as varied interests and abilities.

> The ideal classroom library is organized to inspire readers, is accessible, and encourages students to use it independently.

Think of the classroom library as a physical representation of your beliefs about independent reading and your students' beliefs about themselves as readers.

Classroom libraries have the potential to open up spaces of possibility and understanding about the world in the minds of our students. It is our responsibility to make sure that we have books in which readers can see themselves and learn about a variety of family structures, languages, neighborhoods, religious and cultural traditions, and obstacles that characters face and ways of approaching those obstacles (Laminack and Kelly 2019). When children see themselves reflected in the books they read, their identities are affirmed. "It's not enough to flood them with books of all genres; it's more important to surround them with books that echo their language, their traditions, their ways of being, their ways of dreaming" (Parker 2017, 55).

A 2020 report compiled by the Cooperative Children's Book Center found that 50 percent of children's books featured white people as main characters and another 27 percent featured animals or trucks, while only 10 percent of books featured Black characters, and an even smaller 5 percent featured Latinx characters in central roles. This means that most Black, Indigenous, and People of Color (BIPOC) students are more likely to read books with animal characters than they are likely to read books with characters that look like them. Providing students windows into diverse settings and experiences is equally important in more homogenous classrooms. In order to do this, we need to stay current with new publications and be willing to look at our collections with a critical lens.

Trusting Students to Launch and Maintain the Library

Launching the library alongside your students sends the message that this space belongs to everyone. On the first day of school, there will be several empty shelves, empty baskets, and blank labels. We can almost hear you thinking, "How can I possibly have empty bookshelves on the first day of school?!" or "Won't it look like I just didn't finish setting up my room in time?" We get it. We like neat labels and organization as much as you do! Starting the year by coconstructing the library with your students means releasing some control of your classroom environment; however, it is also an important step in laying a foundation of trust between you and your students. It is a concrete way to say to your new students, "I trust us to do this together and to get to know each other better as we do."

To get started, consider which baskets *need* to be there to support the work of your curriculum. Perhaps you begin your year by studying community. Gather the relevant books in a labeled basket and let this basket be a model. You may have read-alouds that help build a sense of community at the beginning of the year. Put these books on prominent display in the library, creating an enticing example of how collections of books might be celebrated. While the library may seem sparse, keep in mind that putting *too many* books on display right on day one can be intimidating for some students. "We can restrain ourselves from creating a perfectly curated room . . . and have our students walk in, instead, to a blank canvas—a space ready to be transformed slowly, over time, by, with, and for the children in the class" (Hertz and Mraz 2018, 34). Intentionally design the beginning-of-the-year library to serve as a model of possible ways to organize books while leaving space for students to feel a sense of ownership as they start to develop their own plans for the library.

During the first days of school, introduce assortments of books for students to explore. Invite partners

to discuss how these books could be organized in the library. (See page 31's example of a third-grade classroom's chart about organizing its classroom's library.) Which books seem to go together? Why? Are there different ways books could go together? As students decide on categories, provide baskets and labeling supplies, allowing students to make decisions about the precise wording of each label as well as the picture that might best represent that collection.

There are almost limitless possibilities for how students might choose to organize the classroom library. We have worked with some classes who decided to house fiction and nonfiction books about the same topic in a single basket, using a coding system of blue and green stickers to differentiate. Other classes create sections of the library for fiction and others for nonfiction. If you have a bilingual or multilingual library, you may wish to start out by separating your collection while still allowing space for children to assemble a collection of books as they discover connections across texts.

Here are some tried-and-true categories:

- author baskets
- illustrator baskets
- topic baskets
- genre and subgenre baskets:
  - dystopia
  - mystery
  - realistic fiction
  - biography
  - historical fiction
- books for partners and clubs
- favorite character baskets
- series baskets
- class read-alouds

Graphic novels are popular and inspire many students to engage with more challenging texts. Keep in mind that graphic novels are not a genre of books; rather, they are a format that spans many different genres.

The purpose is to involve students in the decision-making, not to make the categories technically "correct." For example, fifth graders might discuss all the ways to organize fantasy books. Do the fantasies that are graphic novels go in a separate basket? Do dystopian books go together, or should fantasy be grouped by setting? You can use this time to kidwatch and facilitate, gaining insights into students' knowledge of authors, genres, and topics, as well as how students work together. Here's an example of a third-grade classroom's chart about organizing its classroom's library.

As the year progresses and students broaden their book choices, they may start to view books in unique ways and then create collections that bring fresh life and whimsy to the library. Tammy Mulligan and Clare Landrigan (2019) share a few new book basket labels created solely by children: "Looking for an Adventure," "Girl Power," "Books to Take Your Mind off Your Worries," "LOL," "Dynamic Duos," and "Parents Lose It." Yet another way to continue to construct the library collaboratively is to conduct a whole-class inquiry connecting the library and book choice. When we ask students, "What do readers think about when they select books?" we uncover how students make these decisions and reveal possibilities for organizing the library in student-centered ways.

Be Mindful About Levels

A discussion about the classroom library would be incomplete without a discussion about the role and use of leveled texts. Fountas and Pinnell (2017) adapted Marie Clay's system of levels as a way for teachers to understand how texts progress in complexity and the ways we can effectively teach readers to word solve, read fluently, and make meaning in increasingly challenging levels. In order to confer effectively, teachers need to understand the nuances of text characteristics and appropriate strategies at each level. This understanding allows us to confer about books we have not read; if we know how books *work* at certain levels, we are better able to ask questions and listen to student responses for instructional implications.

To ensure that students select books within a desired range of accuracy, some schools use levels as a way of organizing both books and children. The unintended consequences of this use of levels are grave. In libraries that are organized by level, it might appear that students have choice; they can select any book from within a particular range of levels as determined by the teacher. This is not choice. This is a system that denies students the opportunity to select books that fit their interests and reading identities and defines students as a level. Fountas and Pinnell have been vocal in clarifying the intended purpose as well as the misuse of text levels. In a blog post on the Fountas and Pinnell website, a text gradient (leveling system) is clarified as a tool for analyzing texts, recording progress over time, and picking books for small-group instruction. Levels are for books, not for readers (Backman 2016).

In the classroom, we can use running records to gather information about a student's strengths and opportunities for growth within a specific level of text, helping to determine which sorts of texts the reader will be able to read with maximum success and independence. We can use this information to group students and to pick appropriate books for guided reading. We can use this information to *guide* a student in making book choices by both being aware of the level of complexity ourselves and, when

Using Book Levels Appropriately	
Use Levels to . . .	**Avoid Using Levels to . . .**
Guide a student in picking books (thinking about challenge and level of difficulty).	Label a student.
Plan guided reading.	Label a basket or book.
Prepare for conferences.	Limit a student's book choices.
Analyze unfamiliar texts.	Always put the same students in a group.
Monitor progress or determine if a student is meeting grade-level expectations.	Label students as high or low.

appropriate, discussing the level of complexity and related useful strategies with the student. We do not want to use levels to *limit* or *define* what a child can read or what texts might satisfy their personal reading identity. The chart above illustrates how to harness the power of levels.

Keeping the Classroom Library Vibrant Across the Year

One way to continuously breathe life into your classroom library is to bring books out at different times of the year. Consider putting aside books that fall into the following categories:

- Books that relate to an upcoming unit of study.
- Books that relate to an upcoming content area unit or author study.
- Books that fall far outside the class' general range of independent reading levels.

Make the most of bringing these books out when the time is right. One fun idea is to use old shipping boxes and wrapping paper to gift wrap the books to be added into the library. Leave the gift-wrapped box on the rug in your meeting area, ready for students to discover in the morning. We promise that if you open it with enough flair, students will be itching to dive right in and begin the work of talking through how and where this new collection could fit into their library as well as the collective reading identity of the class.

Creating opportunities for students to have a say in what books are purchased for the classroom library also creates a sense of ownership, nurturing engagement. Instead of adults making all the decisions, imagine what could happen if we gave students a role in selecting the titles that got added to their classroom libraries. In order to do this, you might place a suggestions box in your library for your students to share ideas for new titles, topics, or authors. Or you might partner with the school librarian, asking them to preview new books with your class and then asking students which titles sparked their interest. We visited one school where the kindergarten teacher routinely displayed the Scholastic book club flyer and had his students discuss their choices for new books. When the books selected by students arrived, the excitement in the classroom created an extended buzz that brought new life to independent reading.

Allowing students more space to talk about and share their reading preferences also creates the authentic need for new library collections. In one first-grade classroom where we worked, students formed their own reading partnerships based on shared interests in common texts. This inspired a new basket labeled "Books for Partners," which contained a variety of titles in sets of two. Other children, who had originally read by themselves at their seats, discovered a mutual love of the Rainbow Magic Fairies series, and a student-centered book club was born. In a fifth grade at the same school, a group of students formed their own book club to read novels by Jason Reynolds around social issues.

What's the best that could happen if we trusted students to organize the classroom library? Your students will grow across the year to become the types of readers who know the reading identities of their friends and regularly recommend books to one another. They will become the kinds of readers who are inspired to dig into a new kind of book, just because the basket was organized by and highly recommended by a friend. They will become the kind of reading community that remains engaged and excited about books.

As children enter our classrooms, we can treat the classroom library as a collaboratively constructed space to send the message that this learning environment values their agency and independence as learners. The act of involving students in the decision-making and valuing their opinions while working together to create a key classroom space shows students that we trust them. When classroom libraries are organized for and by students, these spaces are more likely to both entice students to engage with them and support students' development as readers.

How Book Choice Supports Independent Reading: Balancing Engagement and Accuracy

One of the principles of independent reading is student choice; however, providing students with choice does not mean that teachers cannot influence text selections. We can get started by providing students with routine access to the classroom library. Our youngest readers need a weekly opportunity to select new books, although they may also want to keep a couple of favorites from week to week. Older readers may be ready for a less routine system, meaning that they can visit the classroom library as needed. Most teachers

use book bags, book boxes, or book stacks for students to store their independent reading materials. Ensuring that students have access to these materials throughout the day is an easy way to encourage positive voracious independent reading habits.

As experts in our craft, teachers know that the balance between engagement and accuracy is key to growth (Mulligan and Landrigan 2018). And while a balance of accuracy and engagement is ideal, searching solely for texts that check *both* of these boxes may be too much of a needle-in-the-haystack situation. Instead, guide students toward looking at all their text selections *holistically*. Perhaps a student has several books within a range of leveled texts that they can read independently with a high degree of accuracy, while a few other selections represent easier familiar reads or texts that are difficult but wildly engaging. As students come to know and understand their own identities as readers, they can make text selections that strike a balance between accuracy and engagement more independently and with a greater degree of intentionality.

Finally, we want to ensure that our students are reading in volume. Reading in volume is linked to greater reading achievement and increased oral reading fluency (Allington 2014). When younger students have a variety of texts, they are more likely to stay engaged with their reading for longer stretches of time. Simply put in the words of one of our students: "Having more books I want to read means that I will read for a longer time." As readers are able to engage with increasingly complex texts with greater independence, they typically require fewer books to sustain their independent reading across a week, yet they can still benefit from having a variety of texts. Of course, you may have more voracious readers who require more books and some who are happier with fewer. This is not a perfect science; rather, it is about working alongside students to find a sweet spot that invites maximum levels of engagement and still considers the importance of reading with accuracy. Figuring out the right number of books for a student each week is about drawing on what we know about texts and readers to find balance.

Navigating the Quandary of the Just-Right Book

The messages we send about book choice impact a student's identity as a reader. When we tell students that their just-right books are those that are a particular level, we are narrowing the definition of just-right, and we run the risk of narrowing students' visions of themselves as readers. Supporting students as they explore a wide variety of ways to select books and encouraging the habit of engaging with text for a variety of purposes support and expand their reading identities instead of shutting them down. The following are examples of how to help students think about their reading identities.

How do we pick books?

Look at
the pictures

ASK
A
FroND

BuKs ubiXawT
Anumls

ReeD
ThD
WrooS

FUNNY
PiCtrs

iNTERSTiNG

How do I know if a book is just right for me?

I like it.   Ella

I know the words.   Miguel

It feels good.   Shaquan

I laugh a lot.   Kahleel

The pictures tell me the words.   Jayden

I can figure out the words.   Abby

One common and problematic method for teaching students how to choose just-right books independently is known as the five-finger rule. With this method, the student reads the book and stops to put up a finger each time they do not know a word. If they get to five, this means the book is too hard. Although the five-finger rule seems as if it empowers the student to be agentive in choosing books on their own, it is problematic for a number of reasons. First, this method focuses solely on the student's ability to decode words, elevating decoding over comprehension and reducing reading to an exercise in word calling, not meaning making. Further, this method does not consider other aspects of a student's reading identity, such as background knowledge, interest, or ability to comprehend the text.

While accuracy is, of course, a key factor, we advocate for a broader vision of what just-right might mean to students.

There is ample research that supports the need for students to select books they can read with at least 98 percent accuracy (Allington and Gabriel 2012). Reading with accuracy is essential for increased achievement. However, researchers also agree that engagement is a critical factor for growing strong readers. Students who demonstrate high levels of reading engagement are more likely to transfer classroom experiences with text into actual learning. If you are picturing your students right now, you know as well as we do that books students can read with 98 percent accuracy are not always the books they gravitate toward or find engaging. So how is it that we encourage students to select texts that balance the need for both accuracy and engagement? While accuracy is, of course, a key factor, we advocate for a broader vision of what *just-right* might mean to students. Perhaps a just-right book is one that satisfies their love of a specific topic or author, or it might be a text that speaks to some key aspect of their identity. By expanding the definition of *just right*, we are better able to strike a balance between accuracy and engagement and therefore provide students with the wide choice they crave and deserve.

In the following section, we discuss how you might use reading identity as a way to expand notions of just-right text selections.

Using Reading Identity to Drive Book Choice

Choice has been established as a key factor in the motivation and engagement of students as readers. When students are excited about their reading, they are more likely to dive deeply into the work of making meaning and read for longer stretches of time. And while engagement is a necessity, we also know that children need to spend time in books that they can read with accuracy in order to develop their ability to interact successfully with print. There are a multitude of authentic ways to guide students in how to select engaging independent reading material. Here are a few ideas:

- Model selecting a new book for yourself while thinking aloud about factors such as the book's topic, author, or genre and its readability.
- Explore the power of the blurbs on the backs of books, discussing which books pique your interest and why.
- Encourage students to recommend and share their favorite books through regular book talks.

Perhaps the most empowering way is to approach book choice through a whole-class inquiry into ways that readers choose books. We discuss this inquiry, along with others, in more depth in Chapter 7.

Each of these ways highlights how we might guide students to use the lens of reading identity to make wise, just-right-for-them book selections. Choosing books in these ways reinforces the notion that reading is a joyful, meaning-making process. The following chart illustrates some of these possibilities.

Reading Identity and Book Choice		
Aspect of Reading Identity	Questions It Inspires	How It Can Broaden Book Choice
Attitude	• What kinds of books make you feel excited to read? • How does reading make you feel? • What kinds of texts engage you as a reader? • What topics pique your interest?	• Considering a student's attitude helps to begin a conversation about engagement and the quest to find and expand what makes for engaging material. • Discussing attitude connects how we feel about reading to the choices we make as readers.
Self-efficacy	• Why do you feel confident about this choice? • What is your plan for this book? • Does this book fit your purpose for reading today?	• Considering self-efficacy highlights a student's sense of purpose before starting a book. • Discussing self-efficacy connects what we hope to get out of a book with the choices we make as readers.

continues

Reading Identity and Book Choice, *continued*

Aspect of Reading Identity	Questions It Inspires	How It Can Broaden Book Choice
Habits	• Why do you read? • How do when and where you read affect what you read? • How do you prefer to read—alone or with a partner? • What do you like to do when you are finished with a book? How do you prefer to share your thinking?	• Considering a student's habits also highlights their current purposes for reading. In addition, these questions stress that our purposes for reading flex across setting and time. • Discussing habits uncovers what students are already doing as well as directions for future possibilities.
Book choice	• How do you choose books? • What do you think about when you choose books? • How many books do you like to have at the ready? • What topics or themes are you curious about?	• Considering already established notions about book choice is another entry point for uncovering what students can already do as readers, indicating jumping-off points for future possibilities.
Process	• What is your plan for solving new words in this book? • How do you know if you understand what you're reading? • Does this book represent a challenge for you or something else?	• Considering a student's sense of successful process highlights the strategies they might transfer to make meaning from text. • Discussions of process highlight the importance of both accuracy and meaning making.

Considering how reading identity can influence book choices broadens the notion of what makes a just-right book by emphasizing the notion that a book might be just right for a reader for a number of reasons. In addition, using reading identity as an entry point for these conversations naturally leads to how a student's entire identity might impact their book choice. We read books to see and be seen. Sometimes a book is right because it provides us insight into the experiences of others or helps us to see ourselves validated in the world of print. Rudine Sims Bishop (1990) proposed the idea of books as mirrors, windows, and sliding glass doors, a concept that beautifully illustrates how books can be just right because they speak to our curiosity about ourselves, others, and who we have the possibility of becoming.

How Classroom Routines Support Independent Reading

There are few things most teachers love more than a solid routine. Students thrive when they know what to expect and are trusted to handle the routines of the school day with confidence. Consistent classroom routines allow students to do their best work while also providing a predictable structure that allows for maximum independence.

The most successful routines are clear, are efficient, and enhance learning time while still providing space for student participation. Coconstructing transitions and expectations for transitions alongside your students helps to ensure that these moments do not become about compliance, but rather about the agreed-upon ways in which classroom life flows. Transitions that students can conduct independently also allow the teacher time to circulate and provide specific feedback to those who need it in order to keep transition time positive and quick.

Transitions That Preserve and Enhance Independent Reading

Efficient routines build a sense of mutual trust; teachers and students trust that they are where they need to be at this moment. Routines for transitions make it possible for students to move confidently from one learning experience to the next and for you to devote your time and energy to reading instruction. The following are a few routines related to transitions that support independent reading by creating spaces for agency while also protecting classroom minutes dedicated to reading:

- *Transitioning to independent reading:* Students typically move from a whole-class meeting area to independent reading spots. This transition in particular has great potential to set children up for independent success while still maximizing reading time. Consider creating space for students to manage their own materials, such as book bags or boxes, rather than controlling the distribution yourself. Another option is to assign a student helper, freeing you up to get ready to support readers. Finally, think about how self-selected reading spots around the classroom might foster engagement, habits, and a sense of self-efficacy.

- *Transitioning to partner time:* In Chapter 1, we talked about the variety of ways you might establish partnerships throughout the year. Partner time may happen at the beginning, in the middle, or at the end of independent reading time. Students need to know who their partner is, where they will sit, and a variety of ways of working together. When the logistics of partner time work seamlessly, partners can engage in purposeful reading work together while you give feedback.

- *Transitioning from one book to another:* Finishing a book is not the same as being done with a book. Make this distinction for your readers. *Finishing* a book means it has been read, but perhaps there is more work to do such as talking with a partner or writing a response. Yet, when readers are *done* with a book, it is time to put it back on the shelf, for now, and move on with their reading. Hold class discussions about the numerous options for what readers can do when they are done with a book. Here are a few possibilities:

  - Teach readers how to move from one text to the next, and encourage rereading entire texts or particular sections.

  - Create a library policy for older students to select new texts as needed.

  - Teach into how to create an "up next" pile of books so that new material is ready to go.

  - Provide and teach into how readers might respond to their reading through pictures, reading journal entries, conversations with partners, or reviews.

When you are "finished" with a book, you can...

get another book

talk to a friend about the book

re-read your favorite parts

write about it

Take a moment to imagine what's the best that could happen if you involved your students in the creation and maintenance of these routines. Opening up possibilities for students to have more choice and voice in these logistics sends a clear message about the coconstructed nature of the classroom as well as your belief in student agency. Reimagining classroom routines is one way to trust students to take ownership of classroom life and their own learning.

How the Classroom Environment Supports Independent Reading

We love spending time in teachers' classrooms. The creativity and personal touches in each room help bring instruction to life and create unique spaces that are filled with potential. Of course, the classroom environment is about so much more than color-coordinated bulletin boards and neatly arranged shelves (although those are certainly lovely). Each classroom environment can be intentionally designed to reflect the values that support robust independent reading work: engagement, agency, choice, and joy.

Intentionality and restraint are key here. We want our classrooms to be done on day one; many of us are familiar with daydreams of color-coordinated, neat and tidy classrooms worthy of thousands of social media likes. Yet, despite the best of intentions, these classrooms can send unintended messages to students. When all the aspects of the classroom environment are predetermined and completed by the teacher away from the students, spaces of possibility are shut down. We want to empower our classrooms to be student spaces—classrooms created for, by, and with students in mind.

Reflecting on the Classroom Environment

Aspect of a Classroom Environment	What It Conveys to Students
• *Walls:* Colorful walls are filled with inspirational messages.	• The teacher is the sole source of inspiration and motivation.
• *Library:* Classroom library is fully organized.	• The library is there for students to use, but it belongs to the teacher.
• *Materials:* Student materials are labeled and set out.	• These materials are here for students to borrow, and the teacher will control how and when they are used.

continues

Aspect of a Classroom Environment	What It Conveys to Students
• *Learning artifacts:* Premade charts share learning from an upcoming unit.	• The teacher constructs and captures knowledge for students.
• *Walls:* Walls are mostly empty except for a simple welcome message.	• What do we want our classroom to look like? We can all inspire and motivate each other.
• *Library:* There's a clear space for the classroom library with a few baskets of curated titles.	• How should our library work? We can all see ourselves reflected in this shared library space.
• *Materials:* A variety of paper and writing tools are located in an accessible area.	• What are the possibilities for our materials? We can make decisions about the tools we need and how to use them.
• *Learning artifacts:* There are charts with questions and plenty of blank space.	• How can we construct and capture our learning together? We can all contribute to building new understandings together.

In addition to the classroom library, two other aspects of the classroom environment can support independent reading: anchor charts and student work.

Anchor Charts

Anchor charts are powerful teaching and learning tools. When they are constructed with students, anchor charts provide a way to make learning visible in real time. Once your class has created a chart, you can demonstrate for students how they can use it independently. Refer to the charts often during whole-class discussions and conferences. Anchor charts reflect the knowledge being constructed in the classroom and provide tools to foster greater transfer and independence.

Making your anchor charts dynamic and unique with the help of students ensures that the charts will not merely become wallpaper. Here are a few possibilities:

- *Student-created charts:* Individual students, partners, or groups capture their learning on an anchor chart to share with the class. This empowers them to determine *what* to include and *how* to organize information, while it provides teachers with an opportunity to kidwatch.

- *Interactive writing opportunities:* Construct the chart together through interactive writing.

- *Visually dynamic charts:* Include visuals, such as classroom photos, quick sketches, printed images, or student samples, to make charts accessible and appealing. Anchor charts do not always need to be large; they can be pocket-size, minibooks, or table tents.

- *Multilingual charts:* Create anchor charts in multiple languages, ensuring that they are meaningful to and support the independence of all students.

Be sure to clarify the purpose of each chart. Charts can serve several purposes: to capture routines, to record strategies, to illustrate a process, to be an exemplar, or to define a genre (Martinelli and Mraz 2012).

Student Work

Celebrating student work by posting it on the classroom walls reflects our trust in students and their capabilities. We are sending the message that we value risk-taking and thinking, place more importance on process than product, and are all in this together, working to construct meaning. Showcasing is not about sharing perfect, finalized copies or about communicating current learning experiences to outsiders. Intentionally selected student work should help to drive student independence by elevating strengths, providing models, and establishing goals.

Student Work and Independent Reading		
Type of Student Work	**Purpose**	**How It Supports Independent Reading**
Reading responses	• Reading responses capture student thinking about a text either before, during, or after reading. • Responses can be spontaneous and student-initiated or result from teacher invitations.	• Reading responses share thinking across the classroom community, allowing students another option in addition to class discussion. • Reading responses can serve as models for independent readers and inspire new ways of making meaning.

continues

Type of Student Work	Purpose	How It Supports Independent Reading
Student reflections	• Student reflections capture how students applied various classroom experiences to independent practice. • Reflections support and extend the work of transfer talk.	• Student reflections share different ways of thinking and meaning making across the classroom. • Reflections can encourage students to try new strategies.
Book logs	• Book logs capture quantitative data about readers' independent habits. They can include book titles, genres, page numbers, and number of minutes spent reading. • When used for specific purposes over defined, short periods of time, book logs can provide insight into readers' habits for the teacher and can serve as jumping-off points for student self-reflection.	• Book logs make public the habits of readers and highlight trends happening across the class. Hot titles, favorite authors, and preferred genres all may come to light through this exercise. • Book logs can inspire readers to purposefully try a new genre, try a new title, or connect to another reader.

Trust Your Classroom

We send students messages about what we value the moment they walk into a classroom space. Classrooms that are created collaboratively with students have the power to become joyful and dynamic spaces that foster independence and agency. What is the best that could happen if your classroom began as a blank canvas?

Trust the Data, Big and Small

Instructional Decision-Making

If you don't lead by small data, you will be led by big data.

—Pasi Sahlberg

Here we go again. It's *that* meeting. The data meeting. You know, the one where you sit in front of a huge wall covered in colored squares, each of which contains the name and approximate achievement score of a student. The wall is (apparently) supposed to *speak to you* and help you make instructional decisions. Instead, it serves to strike panic and sometimes shame into your heart. Everything about this meeting feels far removed from the students who sit in front of you every day; this data does not tell the whole story of your class. Just naming a student as "being in the red" leaves out a number of other key pieces of information such as the fact that that same student knows everything there is to know about ocean life and can connect his reading to previous learning yet suffers from a low sense of self-efficacy when it comes to solving the words on the page. Analyzing data points in isolation does not provide a clear path for next steps nor an authentic picture of the whole child.

The reality is that many teachers are overwhelmed by the enormous amount of data they are required to collect and do not have the time to synthesize and interpret it in meaningful ways. From the perspective of the overwhelmed teacher, data collection gets in the way of instruction instead of informing instruction. It is simply exhausting. However, there are meaningful ways of collecting, analyzing, and acting on data that empower teachers and give them a way to uncover the stories of students.

Despite the data demands made by many administrations, Hamilton et al. (2009), along with common sense, indicate that it's not the quantity of the data that counts, but how we use the information. We would extend this notion to claim that not only is it how we use the information that matters, but also who uses it and for what purposes. Data, such as a benchmark assessment in reading, can quickly become less useful to teachers when the data collected during this assessment is reduced to a single outcome or reading level. Further, a primary goal of data-driven instruction is to avoid teaching students what they already know and focus instead on how to build upon that knowledge in ways to which students will best respond (Nuthall 2007). While using data in instructional decisions with this goal in mind can lead to improved student performance (Wayman 2005; Wayman, Jimerson, and Cho 2012; Wohlstetter, Datnow, and Park 2008), no single assessment can tell educators all they need to know to make well-informed instructional decisions; therefore, it is critical to trust multiple teacher-generated data sources, many of which involve avid kidwatching.

We invite you to work within a paradigm that values *uncovering* students' strengths as readers and relying on these strengths as the starting point for instruction. This paradigm shifts away from a *coverage* approach, which prioritizes getting through curriculum, emphasizes benchmarks, and promotes working through a predetermined list of skills and strategies deemed to be grade-level appropriate.

Working in a Culture of Learning and Professional Reflection

Without a supporting culture of learning and professional reflection, the combination of teachers' constant press of time and unacknowledged implicit bias can result, among other things, in a disconnect between data analysis and data interpretation—for example, a teacher lowering expectations for a student because of an unexamined assumption about his homelife.

We find it helpful to look at data analysis as separate from data interpretation, as collapsing the two yields quick decisions that can often be unconsciously driven by bias. In our work with teachers, we define data *analysis* as the systematic collection and organization of information to describe, evaluate, and condense data. We define data *interpretation*

Dr. Hollie reminds us if we find ourselves thinking in a culturally unresponsive way about a student, we have the power to change our thinking. "You must be aware of your first thoughts . . . with the promise that your first thoughts will not be your last thoughts" (2018, 30).

as making meaning or sense from analyzed data in order to develop an informed conclusion that determines the significance and implications of the data collected. Data analysis, or the quick grouping of children into a category, appears to be more efficient, and so the use of data in schools often stops at analysis. Data interpretation takes more time initially and involves stepping back to look at the entire student to determine how the information should impact our next steps, yet it yields longer-lasting results. The gold standard for data interpretation is for teachers to have the time, support, and capacity to interpret data in ways that empower asset-minded stances toward each child, yielding decisions that encompass all that we know about social-emotional intelligence, the power of engagement and identity work, and best practices in instruction related to specific achievement data. In professional cultures that trust teacher reflection and value the process of uncovering, teachers are encouraged to stick with uncomfortable moments, to think them through, and to call upon the collective expertise of their colleagues when needed.

Looking at Data from a Strengths-Based Perspective

A strengths-based approach to data analysis is one aspect of working toward increased possibilities for all students. Deficit-oriented talk can creep into conversations in ways that might appear to be well intentioned or more efficient. This sort of talk can become a sort of shorthand for teachers, used to quickly reference a child as "struggling" or "low." It is a more joyful experience to use data to celebrate students' strengths as they accumulate across the year and to make a plan to move forward with impact. In the following examples on page 51, we illustrate the differences between a deficit-oriented approach and a strengths-based approach to discussing the same child.

If data *indicates* that any one group of students is consistently behind their peers, and the school concludes that the problem resides in the students themselves, then the school has failed to interpret this data fully or accurately. For example, if data indicates all the boys in a particular class are not reading at benchmark, it doesn't mean the boys themselves are

Examples of Deficit-Oriented and Strengths-Based Talk

Deficit-Oriented	Strengths-Based
"Ali is not interested in reading our guided reading texts. He responds to his reading at a literal level and does not try to answer deeper questions. When he is stuck on a word, he gives up and skips it or guesses."	"Ali likes to read books that his classmates recommend to him. He is able to do a clear summary of the books. He uses some strategies, such as looking at the first letter and skipping and returning, on unknown words."
"Gabriella reads only nonfiction. She won't choose anything else. She spends all her time studying the graphs, charts, and illustrations. I can't get her to talk about anything else!"	"Gabriella is an avid nonfiction reader. She is particularly interested in birds and ocean life. Her strength is studying and making meaning from the visual text features. She often takes what she learns in one text and applies it to the next."

the source of this gap; rather it indicates that current instruction is not meeting their needs and merits further investigation. One step to correcting these sorts of errors in data interpretation is to move toward valuing the process of uncovering strengths by maintaining a strengths-based approach to discussing students and to planning for students' learning, seeing possibilities for everyone.

When I read, I can...

infer how the character feels

think about what the author wants me to know

learn new words (what do they mean?)

Use stratagies to figure out new words

Students Name Their Own Strengths

Big and Small Data Defined

Education borrows the terms *big* and *small data* from the field of data science. In the education world, *big data* refers to large-scale data often collected at the district or state level. Think achievement data, demographic data, or other data collected largely by computers. This data serves as an assessment *of* learning and can help districts look for large-scale trends, but it often has little impact on the day-to-day decisions that affect student learning. It is summative in nature. This is because big data can help us see patterns, or correlations, but does not help us to pinpoint causation. So, while big data can help to determine the *what*, it often lacks the ability to determine the *why*, which is the information needed by teachers to make classroom-level decisions about instruction.

Small data refers to information that comes from in-the-moment observations collected by teachers. Small data typically comes from formative assessment methods. Pasi Sahlberg (2017) dubs small data as "the tiny clues that reveal big trends." These tiny clues reveal patterns of student understanding and misunderstanding at the classroom level, as well as indicating the roots of these patterns. Kidwatching is an essential, time-honored tool for small data collection. "Kidwatching provides a framework for engaging in systematic yet very personalized data collection in all areas of literacy. High-quality kidwatching gives you the information you need to teach effectively (Owocki and Goodman 2002, xii). Other common examples of small data collection methods include conferring notes, running records, reading logs, reading journals, anecdotal notes about talk and engagement, and student self-reflections.

Small data serves as assessment *for* learning as it supports teachers as they make decisions about the day-to-day work happening in classrooms. This is the sort of data that speaks to teachers, particularly when various sources are placed together to render a more complete picture of a child, a small group, or a class. And, when used in specific ways, small data also has the power to serve as an assessment for learning that supports *students* in making choices about their reading work and to construct a more robust sense of their identity as a learner.

School systems measure what they value, and then they work to enhance what they measure (Robinson 2017). Schools too often dictate a host of assessments that leave teachers with little say, space, or choice. However, when teachers are able to trust and interpret authentic and accurate in-the-moment data, looking at data turns into an empowering experience that yields clear implications for next steps in instruction. Doing this work requires differentiating between big and small data, considering carefully the purposes and value of each, and trusting teachers to make informed decisions about the right teaching at the right time for the students in their class. Shifting our thinking so that we see assessment as being *for* learning, as opposed to an evaluation *of* learning, allows us to lead by small data, not be led by it.

Small Data That Makes a Big Impact: Collecting Data on the Whole Child

We find that while mentioning the word *data* in a meeting with teachers is usually greeted with an eye roll or a sigh, teachers do get excited about and crave the small data that informs more meaningful day-to-day decision-making. Not only is small data a more authentic source of information about students, but it also lends itself to data *interpretation*, helping teachers to form a more complete picture of the whole child. There are a variety of ways of collecting this data:

- *Kidwatching* allows teachers to observe students as independent learners in independent action, uncovering what they know and can do.

- *Informal running records* allow teachers to observe and analyze student reading behaviors, looking for patterns of error and examples of strengths.

- *Exit slips* allow teachers to analyze student attempts with new learning and encourage student reflection.

- *Conferring notes* capture teachers' observations and thinking while sitting alongside one reader.

These in-the-moment forms of data give us a glimpse into the working minds of our readers, helping us to determine their strengths and appropriate next steps.

The ASCD Whole Child tenets (ASCD 2020) state that all children should learn in emotionally safe environments in which they receive personalized and challenging instruction that sets them up for future academic success and the ability to participate fully in a global environment. To this, we shout a resounding, "Yes!" In order to provide this level of targeted, effective instruction, teachers need to include in their small data repertoire a variety of tools to gauge two key ingredients that set the tone for robust academic learning: engagement and talk. In the following sections, we outline how teachers might go about collecting small data related to engagement and talk in ways that take care not to overwhelm teachers or students. In addition,

Tips for getting started with kidwatching:

1. At the start of independent reading, give yourself a few minutes to observe with notebook in hand.

2. Notice what kids do and say during the read-aloud, shared reading, or both. Take notes.

3. Take time to gauge engagement (see Online Resource 3.2 for a sample).

these methods provide places for students to contribute directly to the collection and interpretation of this data as a means of ensuring that their voices are positioned to tell their stories.

Gauging Engagement: The Reading Engagement Continuum

Instead of thinking about engagement as an absolute (you either are engaged or you are not), it is helpful to think of it as existing on a continuum. The following chart illustrates what you might observe in the classroom during reading instruction across the literacy block. Some indicators of the levels of engagement are clearly visible and observable; some indicators of levels of engagement are revealed in conversations with students. Noticing and naming where students are on this continuum is a powerful way to inform your interactions and feedback and provides a wide variety of entry points into instruction. If you would like to construct your own definitions and indicators, please refer to our Online Resources for a blank Reading Engagement Continuum (Online Resource 3.1).

Sample Reading Engagement Continuum		
Level of Engagement	**Definition**	**Classroom Indicators**
Disengagement	• When a student is not interacting with text in any observable way.	• A student actively avoids reading by creating distractions, such as bathroom breaks, visits to the nurse, or pencil sharpening. • A student does not focus on reading and may move around the room. • A student talks to peers about topics other than reading. • A student consistently abandons books or is unable to find anything to read. • A student does not participate in whole-class discussions. • A student's reading journal or log is blank.

continues

Level of Engagement	Definition	Classroom Indicators
Behavioral engagement or compliance	• When a student goes through the motions of interacting with text but seems not to be truly making meaning.	• A student sits with a book, occasionally turning pages. • A student reads the entire time yet is unable to talk about their reading in specific ways. • A student restates instruction without yet connecting it to their own reading. • A student acts on the teacher's suggestions for authors and books. • A student fills out a reading log or response questions automatically, lifting little meaning from this work.
Cognitive and emotional engagement	• When a student reads and actively makes meaning from a text, demonstrating a sense of self-efficacy as a reader. • When a student makes their own plans for reading, selecting texts and seeking out books with purpose. • When a student reflects upon their reading, actively building upon one or more aspects of their reading identity. • When a student shows evidence of transferring newly taught skills or strategies into their independent reading, integrating these ideas into their work to make meaning from text.	• A student experiences a sense of urgency to read everything by a specific author or about a particular topic. • A student is eager to share their reading and learning with others. • A student is able to articulate a change in their reading identity or perspective. • A student acts on suggestions for authors and books and also seeks out new authors and books, actively growing a reading identity. • A student's written answers move from response to reflection. • A student is emotionally invested in or connected to their reading.

   Noticing and naming a child's level of engagement with independent reading is a good place to start to make an otherwise abstract idea concrete. Jotting down your observations related to engagement aids in reflection and helps to establish patterns. We can make greater meaning from those observations when we put them side by side with the Reading Engagement Continuum.

By recording detailed notes about book choice, habits, and behaviors, you can create a set of data you can use to interpret current reading engagement in your classroom. When you want to dig further into your tentative interpretations of the data, you can turn to students to uncover further information, using the data to frame specific questions. For example, you might observe that a particular student routinely takes ten minutes to settle down and start reading. Using this data as a jumping-off point for the conversation, you might say, "I noticed last week it took you ten minutes to get settled at the start of independent reading time. Over the week, that is fifty minutes of reading time lost. Can you tell me more about that? How can I help?" When studying each child's engagement deeply, you'll factor in a multitude of observations and conversations with the child related to habits, self-efficacy, attitude, and book choice. For a blank Gauging Engagement Note-Taking Form, refer to Online Resource 3.2.

Setting up the conditions that invite students to be more engaged in their reading is essential. By developing trust through close relationships with students, teachers have the knowledge and opportunity to create the conditions for increased engagement. We can influence a student's level of engagement by allowing them to set their own goals, opening up text choice, providing talk opportunities, and encouraging them to share their reading and learning in ways they find meaningful. All students can be engaged.

Readers who are highly engaged are more likely to demonstrate and call into action a wealth of skills and strategies as they work to make meaning from text. Using the continuum facilitates the work of uncovering what students know while also drawing attention to the need for teachers to intentionally invite children to be engaged readers.

How's my Reading Engagement today?

When I am engaged	When I am disengaged	How I can reengage
I want to keep reading	I don't feel like reading.	Ask a friend to recommend a book.
I want to know what is going to happen.	I don't know what to read.	Try a new genre.
I imagine the whole story in my head.	I am distracted.	Read with a friend.
I want to talk about my book.	I'm not thinking about what I'm reading.	Take a break. Go back to reading.
		Reread a favorite book.
		Find a different reading spot.

Therefore, we invite you to consider gauging student engagement in reading as a starting point to your small data collection. You can monitor this throughout the year, as a student's level of engagement as a reader is fluid.

Noticing and naming a child's level of engagement with independent reading is a first step toward fostering deeper engagement as a reader. Sitting alongside readers during independent reading and listening to them speak about their identities as readers helps us to better understand a student's place on the continuum, yielding clearer implications for future instruction. For example, there are times in which behavioral engagement might mask a lack of cognitive engagement. A student who dutifully follows the routines of independent reading might reveal that they actually dislike reading and do not see a place for it outside of school. Yet in other situations, behavioral engagement might lead to increased cognitive engagement (Fisher, Frey, and Quaglia 2018). In these situations, compliance does not take on such a negative connotation. For example, a student who is not yet independently growing theories about the theme of their reading might, after participating in a few strategy groups, become more engaged with their reading as their sense of self-efficacy and process grows.

Gauging Talk: How Talk Supports the Work of Students and Teachers

One way that readers deepen their engagement with text and potentially inspire one another is to talk about their reading. As mentioned in Chapter 1, talk supports independent reading by building relationships, developing ideas, and sharing perspectives. When kids are buzzing about their reading, that is a sign that independent reading is alive and thriving. As children experience how talk serves to expand their meaning making, they become increasingly aware of the power of their collective talk and, as a result, grow to be more strategic and agentive (Nichols 2019). Sometimes classroom expectations get in the way of authentic talk; if we insist on silence during reading, we might inadvertently be getting in the way of students' natural responses to text.

Talk functions optimally in environments in which trust abounds, and, in turn, talk serves to promote and strengthen trust in the classroom throughout the year. Purposeful talk allows students not only to deepen their interpretation but also to understand multiple perspectives and to strengthen community (Nichols 2019). Talking about independent reading can take a variety of forms, including informal book talks, partner work, book clubs, and whole-group discussions. By making a variety of forms of talk available to our students, we increase the possibility for all learners to share their thinking in ways that are comfortable for them.

Talk is a powerful instructional tool. Studies show that teachers often dominate classroom talk (Fisher, Frey, and Quaglia 2018). Further, in classrooms with high numbers of students living in poverty or high numbers of emergent bilinguals, students are given even fewer opportunities to talk and are asked fewer and easier questions (Lingard, Hayes, and Mills 2003). To ensure that we take full advantage of the power of talk, we first have a responsibility to shift the teacher-student talk ratio so that student voices are the most prevalent. A next step is to evaluate our *habits* of talk, including how we initiate talk, the kinds of talk we encourage, and how we listen to and evaluate student talk.

By allowing an adequate amount of wait time and ample opportunities to practice talking with one another, teachers provide students with the space and trust necessary to allow ideas to flourish. Supporting and growing talk necessitates listening to students carefully, and without judgment, in order to ensure that our instruction around talk builds upon children's strengths and ideas. We want to create space for authentic talk to flourish between students while carefully choosing moments where we can provide feedback that also enriches student talk, leading to new understandings. By listening to and making note of what our students can do *naturally* as they talk about their texts, we can find impactful entry points for our instruction around talk. Further, by noticing the behaviors of our students during these talk opportunities, we can also open up new ways for all students to participate comfortably and constructively.

When we talk about books, we can say...

I want to talk about...	Yo quiero hablar de...
I agree...	Estoy de acuerdo...
I have a new idea...	Tengo una nueva idea...
You made me think about...	Tu me haces recordar...
You made me change my mind...	Tu me hiciste cambiar mi idea...
Can you explain what you mean?	Puedes explicarme?
Here in the book...	Aqui en el libro...

Intentionally engaging classrooms provide opportunities for students to talk and for us to teach students to talk productively throughout the day. During independent reading specifically, talk helps students and teachers in a variety of ways (Frazin and Wischow 2019). For teachers, listening while students talk during independent reading can

- aid in gauging student use and understanding of a variety of skills and strategies;
- help to determine a student's understanding of a particular text; and
- reveal clues regarding a student's level of engagement (see the Sample Reading Engagement Continuum on pages 54–55 for clues to support this work).

By getting out of the way and letting students talk about their work as readers, we are better able to know their identities as readers in specific ways that will inform future instruction.

Talk during independent reading also serves teachers *and* students, as we come together to talk and listen to one another. Talk helps to build social bonds, trust, and a community in which students feel safe to take risks, stretching themselves as readers. Teacher talk and student talk help us to

- bring forward the thinking work of readers through modeling;
- articulate who students are as readers;
- build empathy and understanding of others; and
- create social bonds and a sense of trust.

We can do this vital work one-on-one through conferring or with the entire class as we come together at the end of independent reading.

Finally, talk opportunities during independent reading can serve students as well. For students, rich talk coupled with listening can help them

- deepen their comprehension by adding other points of view to grow ideas bigger than those created in isolation and
- practice academic vocabulary.

Therefore, creating space for partner talk during independent reading or just allowing for student-to-student talk during independent reading allows students to take advantage of these opportunities. Plus, when students talk, we get to listen.

Gauging talk involves taking notes as well. Having a notebook handy at all times allows you to jot down snippets of conversations. In addition, you might also want to track the frequency of student talk. Please refer to Online Resource 3.3, Gauging Talk Note-Taking Forms. This online resource includes three templates you can use to capture key information about student talk in real time. In addition, you can occasionally use a device to audio record student conversations to ponder at a later time. Recording conversations in this way also allows you the option of sharing talk work back with the class to aid in reflection and goals for future talk.

Take notes with a question in mind. Are you interested in how students use talk to deepen comprehension? How students incorporate academic vocabulary into their talk? How they further talk on a particular topic by using specific talk moves? Recording notes with a certain lens or question in mind can ease the work and make talk notes powerful in future instructional decision-making.

Putting Small Data Together: Learning the Story of the Whole Child

The best source of data to uncover the story of each child is the child themselves. Sitting alongside students and taking the time to get to know who they are both in and out of the classroom is crucial to our work as teachers. In the second half of this book, we address the ways in which you might facilitate these conversations with readers through conferring.

Here is a chart that examines various sources of small data, who uses the data, what it reveals, and how that data influences classroom decision-making.

The Who, What, and How of Data			
What Is the Data?	Who Is Using the Data?	What Does the Data Reveal?	How Might the Data Be Used?
Running record	Teacher	• What a student is able to do in terms of word solving, fluency, and comprehension within a specific level of text • How a student applies strategies to make meaning from a text • What strategies transfer into independence across the class	• To help students select texts • To help students set intentions • To identify specific strategy work in word solving or comprehension for individual students, small groups, or minilessons

continues

WhatIs the Data?	Who Is Using the Data?	What Does the Data Reveal?	How Might the Data Be Used?
Book log	Teacher	• Trends in book choice across the class, small groups of students, or individual students • Insight into book choice, habits, volume, stamina, and engagement	• To inform upcoming read-aloud selections or book talks • To support the organization of authentic book clubs or partnerships • To inform intention setting
	Student	• Insight into book choice, habits, volume, stamina, and engagement	• To identify preferences and name them as part of their identity as a reader • To identify reading patterns that may lead to reading intentions
Whole-book assessment (You can create your own or use Jennifer Serravallo's Complete Comprehension series, 2019.)	Teacher	• Ways a student constructs meaning across a whole book	• To help students select texts • To identify patterns across the class • To identify specific future comprehension strategy work for individual students, small groups, or minilessons
	Student	• Insight into their understanding of texts	• To select their new reading intention
Conferring notes	Teacher	• Student strengths • Possibilities for next steps	• To support student intention setting • To inform the work of small groups • To hold up students for their strengths • To inform the work to be done with future read-alouds

continues

What Is the Data?	Who Is Using the Data?	What Does the Data Reveal?	How Might the Data Be Used?
Engagement	Teacher	• Patterns of engagement across the class	• To inspire a whole-class inquiry into reading engagement • To name and celebrate strengths • To determine which students might need support with how to reengage themselves
	Student	• Insights into reading identity: how might these contribute to engagement?	• To collaborate with the teacher to find ways to engage or reengage in reading
Talk	Teacher	• Patterns of talk across the class • Individual students' talk habits	• To inspire whole-class inquiries • To name and celebrate areas of strength • To determine students who might need support with talk
	Student	• How they are contributing to meaning making alongside the class	• To determine accessible entry points into the conversation

Trust Your Data, Big and Small

Collecting data is a fluid, responsive process. We move from assessing through kidwatching, to reflecting on the data that process reveals, to planning instruction with that data in mind, and back again to more kidwatching.

Every teacher needs to find their own way into small data collection methods that work to uncover the story of each class. As you move forward, we invite you to reflect upon these three beliefs about data:

1. There is power in uncovering a more complete story of students by moving beyond data analysis to data interpretation.

2. The use of authentic small data based in avid kidwatching leads to more powerful decision-making.

3. The inclusion of children in the collection of data leads to a more student-centered picture and valuable self-reflection.

Give It a Go: Instructional Decision-Making

There is no one way of gauging engagement or talk. What are you most curious about related to the areas of engagement and talk? Do you want to get a sense of the levels of engagement of the entire class? Do you have one or two students you want to learn more about? You can use the following chart to get started; pick a method that best suits your area of curiosity or your style of teaching.

Method: What You Can Do with the Class	Gauging Engagement: What It Might Sound Like	Gauging Talk: What It Might Sound Like
Give It a Go: Engagement and Talk		
Facilitate a whole-class discussion and take notes.	• What does it mean to be engaged in our reading? • What can we do when we feel disengaged?	• What are the best ways to share our ideas with the class? • How do we decide what ideas we want to pursue? • How can we have a focused conversation about one big idea?
Kidwatch during independent reading.	• Are students engaged in their reading? How do I know? • Are students disengaged or compliant readers right now? How do I know?	• How are students using talk to construct meaning during independent reading? • What talk moves do students rely on?
Kidwatch during other components of balanced literacy.	• Where are students on the engagement continuum during this component? How do I know?	• How are students using talk to make meaning during this component? How do I know? • What does student talk reveal about students' understanding and misunderstandings?
Confer with students.	• Where is this student on the reading engagement continuum in this moment? • Where might the student identify themselves on the engagement continuum?	• How does the student use talk to reflect on their work as a reader?
Analyze written responses or self-reflections.	• Where might the student identify themselves on the engagement continuum? • What does the student know about how to reengage themselves in reading?	• How does the student feel about their own capacity to contribute to whole-class meaning making? • In what ways does the student feel most comfortable contributing to class discussions?

Part Two

Trust Conferring

> Conferring is one of the ways we help children understand that even when they're working alone, they're not alone in the work.
>
> —Debbie Miller

As with independent reading, the benefits of conferring are well established by research. Research strongly suggests there are multiple reasons to confer, including to uncover a reader's attitudes toward reading (Burkins and Yaris 2014), to explore a reader's process and to discover how a reader is interacting with the text (Goldberg 2016; Barnhouse 2014), and to form theories about the work of the reader (Calkins 2015). In the interest of guiding students toward greater independence and growth, conferring must be a central, consistent part of your teaching. James Comer (1980), renowned child psychiatrist, stated that significant learning cannot happen without significant relationships. During conferring, we build relationships and thereby convey to children our confidence that they are capable of taking an active role in their own learning.

The reading conference is a powerful ten-minute investment of time, ripe with the potential for vital relationship building and transformational teaching. In order to teach reading in transformative ways, teachers need to be able to create time and spaces in which both they and their students have agency in their reading work.

Conferring relies on a trusting relationship between student and teacher. Based on the principles of dialogic teaching, it is a regularly occurring conversation between a student and a teacher about, in this case, the student's independent reading. A conference can serve many purposes: getting to know the student's reading identity, collaborating with a student to set goals, and working alongside a student to help them meet those goals.

Imagine the possibilities when conferring honors these well-researched stances and creates spaces for students and teachers to trust the ways in which students construct meaning from text, knowing that the pursuit of these intentions leads to powerful feedback opportunities and, ultimately, reading growth.

Impactful conferring is based on four principles: time, choice, talk, and teacher support.

Time + Choice + Talk + Teacher Support = Impactful Conferring

1. **Time:** Students need and deserve time to discover and pursue their own ways of making meaning and to trust that these purposes for reading are valued. With time, students are able to use their reading to construct and reconstruct their identities, developing their social comprehension as they consider how they relate to others in the world.

Teachers need and deserve the chance to learn the whole stories of their students. Teachers use this time to craft feedback that provides the right teaching at the right time. Further, when students have time to read independently alongside teachers, they are able to build the sorts of trusting relationships that are the foundation for authentic learning.

2. **Choice:** In order to read in agentive ways, students need the freedom to choose their own intentions for reading. In addition, students need opportunities to choose *what* and *how* they want to read, including the ability to decide when to read alone, with a partner, or in a book club. When combined with the time to read widely, these choices are key to increasing a student's motivation, persistence, and growth (Schunk 2003).

   Teachers choose to follow the lead of students by supporting their intentions. During the conference, teachers choose to listen to their students from a strengths-based perspective with the goal of providing feedback.

3. **Talk:** In order to become agentive readers, students need to have a strong voice in the conference. When students can contribute meaningfully to the conference, their understanding and motivation increase.

   Teacher talk, specifically process-oriented questions and feedback, is in the service of supporting students' ways of making meaning. For the teacher, talk is grounded in listening. The teacher uses talk to facilitate, collaborate, or connect with the student. Through talk, students and teachers develop shared understandings of the student's current strengths and determine new pathways for instruction.

4. **Teacher support:** Teacher support is an indispensable component of effective independent reading. Supportive partnerships with teachers and peers yield lifelong readers and long-term student success (NCTE 2019; ILA 2018). Teacher support includes interpreting data, following students' lead, and providing the right teaching at the right time.

   Feedback is an essential piece of teacher support. Research clearly shows that of all the methods of teaching at our disposal, feedback is one of the most powerful influences on learning and achievement (Hattie and Clarke 2019). Specific and consistent feedback allows students to practice reading with a clear understanding of the skills and strategies they are working on. Conferring is the perfect time for teachers to give feedback and to receive feedback from students.

Types of Feedback: Teacher to Student

Feedback can serve a variety of functions. Feedback that names a strength and feedback that names next steps are two clear types of teacher-to-student feedback:

- *Strengths-based feedback* notices and names a strength, serving to reinforce what the student is already doing or attempting to do and encouraging the student to continue to do it.

- *Next-steps feedback* introduces a student to a new strategy or prompts for a not-yet-transferred strategy. The teacher first clearly states the strategy. Then the teacher might ask: "Do you want to give this a go by yourself, do you want me to show you, or do you want to try it together?"

The following a chart illustrates these two types of teacher-to-student feedback.

Two Types of Teacher-to-Student Feedback		
Type of Feedback	**Why We Do It**	**What It Might Sound Like**
Strengths-Based Feedback		
Word-solving strategy	To reinforce a new strength in word solving that you want the reader to continue to use and practice. To reinforce a strength that a student has demonstrated many times, which will be a jumping-off point for your teaching.	"You looked at the picture and you checked the first letter of the word. You put that together to make sure that the word makes sense." "You were able to figure out all those new words. You broke each word into chunks and then put the whole word together."
Comprehension strategy	To reinforce a new strength in comprehension that you want the reader to continue to use and practice. To reinforce a strength that a student has demonstrated many times, which will be a jumping-off point for your teaching.	"You retold the story including the beginning, middle, and end of the story. You included all the important events." "You are thinking a lot about how the characters are complex. You talked about how sometimes the character acts one way, and other times the character acts a different way."

continues

Two Types of Teacher-to-Student Feedback, *continued*		
Type of Feedback	**Why We Do It**	**What It Might Sound Like**
Next-Steps Feedback		
Word-solving strategy	To build upon a student's strength by providing tailored instruction in what comes next for them as a reader. Next steps are tied to a word-solving goal that has been selected by the reader.	"When you are solving words, sometimes you come up with two possibilities that make sense. One thing you might try is to look all the way across the word to the ending sound to see what looks right." "Another way of figuring out a word is to look at the base word and then look at the prefix."
Comprehension strategy	To build upon a student's strength by providing tailored instruction in what comes next for them as a reader. Next steps are tied to a comprehension goal that has been selected by the reader.	"When readers talk about what happened in their stories, they can use transition words like at the beginning or next to make their thinking clearer to the listener." "Another way readers learn about characters is by thinking about how the characters change and what makes them change."

Types of Feedback: Student to Teacher

In order to consistently tailor instruction to meet students' needs, it's important to listen for student-to-teacher feedback. The feedback we receive from students not only communicates their needs but also reveals clues about engagement, understanding, and misconceptions (Hattie and Clarke 2019). This happens in classrooms where trust has been established between student and teacher and among the students themselves.

Students give feedback to teachers in a variety of ways: through body language, behavior, and talk. We need to live our lives in the classroom on the lookout for student feedback and seek out further insight into student understanding through the use of process-oriented questions. Questions such as "Tell me, what are you going to do?" or

"What do you mean by that?" open up space for the student to provide feedback to the teacher. This information allows us to better gauge our impact and make informed decisions about future teaching opportunities.

Avoiding assumptions about the root of students' behavior is essential to truly assessing our impact. For example, if a student rolls their eyes during a conference or is not effusive in answering questions, it may be tempting to be hurt or to make an assumption about the student. However, when we accept this information as feedback from the student, it becomes easier to put our assumptions aside and probe further. In these moments, reflecting on prior teaching yields more positive possibilities than making assumptions about student capabilities.

The Role of Trust in Conferring

In the introduction to Part 1, we defined *trust* as believing that the person who is trusted will do what is expected. Trust is reciprocal; both student and teacher enter into the relationship believing that the other will do as expected. In a conference, students trust that we understand them as readers and will give them the support they need. And we teachers trust that students will come to the conference ready to work and will follow through independently after the conference. We also trust that the rest of the students are, in fact, reading while we focus on one student at a time. Does this mean that every single student is doing the exact right thing for all thirty or forty-five minutes? Of course not. But it means that we trust that students are doing their best to work toward a fuller vision of themselves as readers.

Trusting Teacher-Student Relationships

When we approach students with respect, trust, honesty, and communication, we can build and maintain strong relationships, which, in turn, are a key component to developing engaged, motivated readers (Fisher, Frey, and Quaglia 2018). Central to this relationship building is devoting time to understand and engage with the student's whole self, including their lived experiences both in and out of school. It is by trying to know the story of a child that teachers can harness the power of relationships, trusting that it is the relationship that will aid in the creation of relevant and engaging instructional invitations. Understanding our students' lives outside of school helps us to build a bridge between their learning in school and the potential for its positive impact on their lives outside of school (Minor 2019). It is one way that we ensure that our teaching stays relevant.

Our investment in positive teacher-student relationships contributes not only to growth in all aspects of a student's identity but also to improved academic performance and independence as well (Howard, Milner-McCall, and Howard 2020). Conferring specifically contributes to positive teacher-student relationships because it celebrates student voice, makes conversations about reading more personal, and allows teachers and students to build relationships around books.

The Power of Listening

Listening well is an act of empathy. As the listener, you aim to see the world through another person's eyes with the goal of understanding their perspective (Bryant 2019). Listening empathically means that you are listening with intent, the intent to understand someone else's point of view. This might mean understanding how a student is making meaning from text or it might mean how a student experiences the world.

When we trust our students to lead the way, the art of listening takes on a new importance. There is a vast difference between listening *to* our students and listening *for* our students to make a mistake. On the surface, listening for students to make a mistake seems like a fine path for directing the conference. After all, when a student makes a mistake, we have strategies to teach them how not to make that same mistake again. However, in practice, if we limit ourselves to listening for mistakes, our understanding of the student and our teaching will be limited to the visible parts of reading. When we listen *to* our students as they read and discuss their understanding, we gain insight into the processes that they use to interact with the text; we allow our students to begin to create the path for us to follow.

"Listening is the fundamental frame of reference in a reading conference. The more time we spend listening, the more time the conferee spends talking. The more the conferee talks, the more clarity we have about his reading strengths and growth areas" (Allen 2009, 17).

As we shift into listening *to*, instead of listening *for*, we must also shift our approach to questioning. Consider the difference between answer-driven questions and process-oriented questions. Answer-driven questions are highly related to a specific text. There are right and wrong answers. Typically, answer-driven questions provide limited insight into the processes that readers use to interact with a text. Process-oriented questions yield more opportunities to gain insight into our students' thinking as they work through a text. They also open the door for students to give us feedback. Process-oriented questions demand more of the student. The following chart highlights the difference between the two types of questions.

Answer-Driven Versus Process-Oriented Questions

Answer-Driven Questions	Process-Oriented Questions
What is your favorite book?	Tell me about yourself as a reader.
Which words on this page were challenging?	What challenges you as a reader?
Who is the main character?	What are you paying attention to as you read?
What is the main idea?	What are you wondering about as you read?
What are you reading?	What are you doing as a reader?

When listening, don't be afraid of silence. Students need time to think. Rushing in to "save" them undermines their sense of agency and sends the message that they are not capable of figuring things out independently. This hard-to-break habit contributes to student disengagement and learned helplessness. It is important to linger in the silence, trusting that the student will respond.

An Overview of the Cycle of Conferring

The Cycle of Conferring is a three-part framework that is based on three continuous needs:

- Uncover students' evolving reading identities and strengths.
- Provide space for students to voice their intentions by creating what-if questions to pursue during independent reading.
- Provide feedback to students as they move toward exploring these questions.

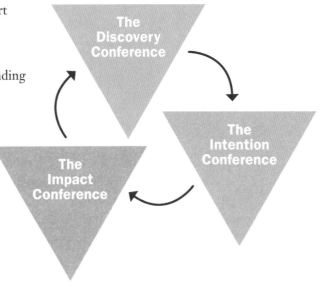

Each conference within the Cycle of Conferring is represented by a triangle that is broad at the top and comes to a point at the bottom. We used this upside-down triangle (although our math brains question whether or not this triangle really qualifies as upside down, but stick with us . . .) to represent the flow of this conference as moving from broad to more specific aspects of reading identity. See? Upside-down triangle. Each conference begins with a broad invitation to the reader to engage, allowing the teacher to meet the reader where they are in their work *at the moment*, ensuring that feedback will be timely and specific to the current needs of the reader (see below).

As you read on, we invite you to imagine new spaces of possibility for yourself and for your students: what is the best that could happen if you devoted time to conferring during independent reading?

The Cycle of Conferring	
Kind of Conference	**Purpose of Conference**
Discovery Conference	In the Discovery Conference, you devote time to uncovering students' reading identities. This information sets you up for the Intention Conference. This part of the cycle typically lasts 1–2 conferences.
Intention Conference	In the Intention Conference, you devote time to uncovering students' authentic intention for meaning making in order to create What If questions to guide independent reading work. Student intentions drive instructional decisions in the Impact Conference. This part of the cycle is typically done in one sitting.
Impact Conference	In the Impact Conference, you devote time to supporting a student's intention by providing tailored instructional feedback. This part of the cycle consists of multiple conferences. This set of conferences ends with a student contribution.

4

Trust Readers to Have a Story

The Discovery Conference

I don't believe there are "struggling" readers, "advanced" readers or "non" readers. . . . I think young people should not be judged by the level of their reading but by the way a book makes them think and feel. By the way it gives them hope. By the way it opens them up to new perspectives and changes them.

—Jacqueline Woodson

Conferring centers the child, allowing students and teachers to co-construct relevant learning pathways. This chapter outlines the first conference in the Cycle of Conferring, during which you devote time to uncovering students' reading identities. This conference positions teachers to trust their students as well as the relationships they have built with students, with an eye toward celebrating student strengths and cultivating joyful reading. As one teacher mused aloud after conducting her first set of Discovery Conferences, "Our teaching of reading has become so narrow we have forgotten to teach our students to love reading." It takes courage to reimagine our teaching so that it centers on trusting our students to know themselves and to be engaged in their own learning. And it takes courage to trust ourselves.

One September, we met Pari, a first grader who was not yet reading conventionally. During the Discovery Conference, when we asked her about reading, she shrugged and said, "I don't like to read. I like playing instead. I like playing princess with my sister." We nodded and then Pari shared with us that she loved to spend time with all the princess books she had at home, but that the books at school were boring. Later, with her classroom teacher, we gathered a number of princess books to share with Pari in the Intention Conference. Her face lit up when she saw them all! While the teacher continued to instruct her using leveled books during guided reading, during independent reading, Pari read her beloved princess books. When we met with her again at the end of the year (by which time she was reading at the first-grade benchmark), she declared, "I love reading!" In second grade, when the class was writing letters, she wrote us a letter about the series books she was reading –still about princesses and fairies.

Reading Identity Defined

Impactful reading instruction starts with getting to know the student's identity as a reader. As we uncover details about their reading identities, we can use this information to ground instruction that is tailored to the needs and identities of each child.

Jan 29   Miss Hannah
Dear
Have you ever heard
of Dark Fairy O
and it is wicked you
should read it. My
favrite chactere is
The Rockin fairy!
whats yours? mabey
you do not have
one I hope
you do.

Pari's Letter to Hannah

Feb. 6
The serires are
soso soso so soso
so so soso sosososo
good I think

you will read. one
of my favrite
serires is the

Dark fairy and
the prinsess of plants
I think you would
read it.
Love Pari

Reading identities shape students' motivation and engagement and can also play a role in how they think and talk about texts. For example, students with positive self-identities are more likely to talk in groups, which, in turn, deepens their comprehension of the text (Hall 2007, 2012). Take a moment and think about your identity as a reader.

Reading identity and reading engagement have a reciprocal relationship.

How do you feel about reading? What has reading been like for you in the past? Where do you like to read? Have you ever read a book you couldn't stop thinking about? What do you think about as you read? How does reading make you feel? Sharing these insights into your own identity is an inviting way to begin the conversation about reading identity with your class.

Reading identity is multifaceted—and impossible to separate from reading engagement. Reading identity and reading engagement have a reciprocal relationship; when a student feels confident in their reading identity, they are more likely to be deeply engaged in their reading. In turn, being deeply engaged with text naturally leads to a stronger positive sense of reading identity. We define reading identity as consisting of the following aspects: attitude, self-efficacy, habits, book choice, and process. Some of these aspects are visible and some are invisible. Many of these aspects overlap and may be evidenced at the same time. When getting to know students as readers, consider how all the aspects of reading identity are interwoven.

Aspects of Reading Identity

Reading identity is not fixed, but fluid and dynamic. As the school year evolves, students' sense of self as readers shift and change. The child who started the year feeling confused when they read longer books ends the year with multiple strategies for tracking plot. The child who picked only nonfiction books in the beginning falls in love with fantasy.

Our role is to uncover, reinforce, expand, and in some cases reframe all aspects of students' reading identities, with the goal of boosting their motivation and, therefore, their success. The following chart defines the five aspects of reading identity: attitude, self-efficacy, habits, book choice, and process. Notice that reading engagement is not a separate component; rather, reading engagement influences all aspects of reading identity.

Reading Identity Defined

Engagement with text is an overarching consideration that spans and interacts with all aspects of students' reading identity.

Aspect	Description

Attitude	A student's attitude toward reading may be positive or negative. It includes the following:
	• how the student feels about reading
	  ○ how the student feels about current reading instruction
	  ○ how the student feels about reading aloud? With a partner? By themselves?

Self-efficacy	A student's sense of self-efficacy encompasses how confident they feel in their own abilities. It includes the following: • how the student perceives themselves as a reader • how the student understands others perceive the student as a reader • how the student perceives interactions with the teacher relative to reading
Habits	Habits include what the student does both in and outside of school. For example, the student might do the following: • read in a preferred spot at home and at school • read outside of school • read for extended periods of time • seek out others to talk about books • draw or read about books • use the library with confidence • make future reading plans • choose to read when given a choice
Book choice	Book choice refers to what a student considers when choosing books. Examples of student considerations include the following: • familiar books • favorite books • author • genre • text type • popularity in the class • series • books that speak to the child's identity • the way the student feels about the books that are suggested by others

continues

Engagement with text is an overarching consideration that spans and interacts with all aspects of students' reading identity.

Aspect	Description

Process	Process is the work a student does independently to solve words, read fluently, and comprehend. It includes the following:
	• word solving
	• fluency
	• comprehension
	    ○ inferring
	    ○ synthesizing
	    ○ monitoring for meaning
	    ○ critiquing
	    ○ questioning
	    ○ visualizing

I'm the kind of reader who...

lafs aand maks it fun for me
reads ih sid and owt sed
likes fune bux

woNders
Tris Toers

reADs The wrts

Who Are We as Readers?

The Discovery Conference: Uncovering a Student's Reading Identity

Each conferring cycle begins with a Discovery Conference. The purpose of the Discovery Conference below is to get to know who our students are as readers. As a result of kid-watching and data collection, you may already have quite a bit of information about this; however, when you take the time to "roam around the known" (Clay 2005, 32) alongside a student, the picture of that student will emerge more clearly. Over the course of the year, you will hold a number of Discovery Conferences with your students, allowing you to get to know and reknow them and their evolving reading identities. Later in the school year, prompt students to reflect on how they might have changed as readers. It can be as simple as adding the word *now* to some of these questions. For example, you might say, "Tell me about yourself as a reader *now*," or "How have you changed as a reader?"

The Discovery Conference

Attitude and self-efficacy

Tell me about yourself as a reader.

Why do you read?

Habits and book choice

How do you pick books?

When and where do you like to read?

Process

What are you doing as a reader?

What are you thinking about as you read?

Please pick a part of your reading to share . . .

Name a strength

"May I tell you something I learned about you as a reader?"

If you have students who are emergent bilinguals, it may be more inviting to conduct this conference in the students' first language, or rely on translanguaging, allowing the students to respond in whichever language(s) they choose.

The Discovery Conference is a conversation that lasts five to ten minutes with each child. The conference is divided into three sections, each of which is designed to uncover and then highlight a particular aspect of a student's reading identity. You can use Online Resource 4.1, Discovery Conference Template (shown below), to take notes during the Discovery Conference. This template provides prompts, space for note-taking, and space for quick reflections immediately following the conference. Tailor the questions to match what you already know about the student as a reader, and ask natural follow-up questions.

The first item on the template is overall engagement. There is no single question that gauges engagement; use the Reading Engagement Continuum (Online Resource 3.1), your kidwatching notes, and what you learn in the Discovery Conference to reflect on the overall engagement of the student either before, during, or after the conference.

Name: _____	Date: _____	Grade: _____
Discovery Conference Template		
Overall engagement		
Attitude and self-efficacy	Tell me about yourself as a reader. *Possible prompts (if needed):* • I'm the kind of reader who . . . • How do you feel about yourself as a reader? • How do you feel about reading at school? • How do you feel about reading at home? • Why do you read?	

continues

Discovery Conference Template, *continued*

Habits and book choice	Tell me about when and where you like to read and how you choose books. *Possible prompts (if needed):* • When and where do you like to read at school? At home? • What do you think about when you pick books? • Do you have any favorites? • With whom do you read? • What makes you stick with a book? • Have you ever stopped reading a book before you finished? Why? • *[If a child is in the midst of reading]* Why did you pick *this* book?	
Process	Tell me what you are thinking about or paying attention to as you read. *Possible prompts (if needed):* • How do you know you are understanding what you read? • How do you figure out words? • What do you do when you don't know a word? • What do you know about this book so far? What are you thinking about?	
Name a strength	*Possible prompts (if needed):* • May I tell you about one of your strengths as a reader? • May I tell you something you are doing well? • This is what I learned about you as a reader. • I noticed that as a reader, you . . .	

Reflections

What did I learn about this reader?	What am I left wondering about for this reader?	What are possible next steps?

Here are some tips to make the conference go smoothly:

- *Be prepared.* Have note-taking forms copied and ready. Have your favorite pen on hand. Make sure to have sticky notes or index cards if you decide to leave an artifact with the student.

- *Accept all of the student's answers without judgment.* Check your biases. There are no right or wrong answers. Everything that the student says is valuable.

- *Listen and provide wait time.* Listen to the student to learn about them and from them. Wait; leave spaces long enough for the student to think, respond, and then add onto that response if desired.

- *Probe for further information if needed.* Trust yourself to come up with natural follow-up questions. Use prompts such as "Tell me more" or "Say more about that" to encourage students to share more.

- *Take notes as you go or make a recording.* Capturing the student's exact words or phrases is helpful, as their words give us insight into their ways of thinking. We can use these words as a bridge in future instruction, providing more academic vocabulary when appropriate. Also, taking notes allows us to refer to this small data throughout the conferring process and the school year.

As with many aspects of teaching, the conference may not always go the way we imagine it. If you feel anxious after a conference seems to go awry, remember: action is the antidote to anxiety. It is in these moments that we have to trust the power of following our students' leads. These seemingly baffling conversations may reveal more than you initially think once you take time to reflect on the student's answers and contemplate possible next steps. Some students may say that they love books that remind them of home, and others may share, "I like Elephant and Piggie books." Both of these comments reveal insights into how the students construct themselves as readers. This is our starting place for instruction.

Naming Students' Strengths

Naming strengths provides powerful and specific feedback that reinforces strategies students have transferred to independent work. The Discovery Conference ends with the teacher naming a specific strength or new learning about the student as a reader. This not only helps to build a positive relationship but also serves future reading work by bolstering confidence.

We offset this final piece of the conference by saying something like, "May I tell you about one of your strengths as a reader?" These seemingly simple phrases catch students' attention and prepare them to receive positive feedback. Students sit a little taller and smile when they hear us say this. The following chart illustrates ways of naming strengths that highlight various aspects of reading identity.

Naming Strengths		
Student Comment	Aspect(s) of Identity or Engagement You Want to Highlight	What You Might Say
"Every night I choose a book to read out loud to my little sister."	• habits • engagement	"You're the kind of reader who finds lots of different times and reasons to read. I know from watching you in school that you like to read by yourself and I just learned that at home, you read to your sister."
"I don't like graphic novels. I read them because everyone else in the class is reading them. I really like nonfiction, like about sports."	• attitude • book choice	"You're the kind of reader who knows what you like and don't like. Readers can't all like the same thing. We can use your love of nonfiction to help you choose books that are interesting to you."
"I love the Sofia Martinez books, so I collected them all. I want to start my own book club."	• habits • book choice	"Right now, you're the kind of reader who knows that reading is not always something you want to do by yourself. Starting a club is a great way to really enjoy and share favorite books."
"I love *The Parker Inheritance*, but it is confusing. I'm not that good a reader. There's a lot of stuff going on. I fold down a page when I don't understand, so I can go back to it."	• self-efficacy • process	"I learned that you focus on the plot when you read. You stick with a book, even when it gets confusing, and you have come up with a strategy to help yourself understand."
"Here is my book box. I am reading this book right now, but when I get tired, I also have books for taking a break."	• engagement • habits	"I learned that you know how to keep yourself engaged in your reading by changing the books you read to match what you feel like reading in that moment."
"This book has so many characters! I am using sticky notes to mark when I learn something new about the main characters."	• process • engagement	"I noticed that in the kinds of books you're reading now, there are many characters to keep track of. On your own, you chose one of the strategies we have used in class before as a great way to not get lost."

Here are some tips for naming strengths:

- *Remember that language matters.* Notice we do not name a strength by saying, "I love that you . . ." This is praise, which undermines a student's sense of agency and leads to increased teacher dependence. Instead, we clearly name what the student is doing by using stems such as these:

    - One of your strengths as a reader is . . .

    - I notice that you . . .

    - You are the kind of reader who . . .

    - Right now, when you read, you like to . . .

    - I just learned that . . .

    This language clarifies what it is the student has done successfully, as opposed to praising what they did. We want to position strengths as part of the student's reading identity that the student can call on again.

- *Think beyond skills.* Imagine spaces of possibility to highlight *all* aspects of a student's identity (both the visible and the invisible). The visible pieces of reading work typically refer to the print work and decoding; stretch yourself to give compliments that acknowledge aspects of a student's identity that typically receive less attention, such as habits, attitude, and book choice. Here are some compliments to try out:

    - Name a newly revealed aspect of their identity.

    - Name an aspect of the student's identity that you want them to feel more confident about.

    - Notice how a student has transferred whole-class teaching or a previous goal to their independent reading.

    - Use the student's words whenever possible.

To make these strengths visible and transferable for the student, leave behind some sort of concrete reminder. These reminders are most meaningful when they are created alongside the student, in the moment. You might give the child a sticky note to put on the front of the book or book box. Another option is to add a series of these reminders to a class chart, honoring the strengths of all students publicly and in ways that may encourage productive partnerships or students seeking out other students as experts rather than relying solely on the teacher. Highlighting strengths through physical reminders sends a clear message that students can trust teachers to see them fully, not just focus on areas of struggle. See the following examples of concrete reminders.

Right: A kindergarten student talked about how he knew that his books had patterns and that the patterns helped him know what each page said. This is the reminder that highlighted his use of strategies related to process.

You use patterns!
△○□△○□

We are readers!

I can use the picture.

I can tell a story.

I can read a book again. (2x)

I can read with a friend.

I can treat books with ♥. ♥

I can talk about my book.

You are the kind of reader who looks for connections across books! ☺

Above: A third-grade student shared that many of her books were about the conflicts that occur in friendships. She noticed that most of these conflicts were resolved. This is a sticky note that highlighted her use of process.

Above: This chart, created in a first-grade classroom, highlights various strengths related to the processes students in the class were relying on while engaging with emergent text.

Right: This chart of reading strengths, created in a fourth-grade class, highlights what students were thinking about as they read.

Our strengths as readers...

★ ...figuring out WHY and HOW characters change.
- Charles
- Lily
- Jasmine

★ ...reading a new GENRE
- Sebastian
- Koran

★ ...thinking about the LESSON or MESSAGE
- James
- Malik
- Ferissa

★ ...asking QUESTIONS while reading.
- Elizabeth
- Blake

After the Discovery Conference, give yourself time to reflect: read your notes and consider what you have learned, putting this new information next to other data you have about the child. By combining all you know about the child with your literacy expertise, you can begin to contemplate possible goals for the child. This reflection work is the bridge to the Intention Conference.

For reflection, we suggest three key questions to guide your thinking:

1. What did I learn about this reader?

2. What am I still wondering about this reader?

3. What are possible next steps?

The Discovery Conference Template (Online Resource 4.1) includes a space to do this work immediately following the conference.

The Discovery Conference in Action: The Stories of Three Readers

Following are three common scenarios for the Discovery Conference based on our work with students. When we met them, each of these students was in a different place along the Reading Engagement Continuum. These scenarios illustrate how we went about uncovering their reading identities. After each scenario, we walk you through our thought process and initial steps in preparing for the upcoming Intention Conference. As you read these scenarios, picture one of your own students who might currently display similar dispositions.

Scenario One: Emily's Story

In this scenario, Jen conferred with Emily, a second-grade student who always had her head in a book and displayed visible signs of engagement with her independent reading, such as using the classroom library independently and reading for long periods of time. Sometimes she didn't even hear the teacher saying that reading time was over.

Jen: Tell me about yourself as a reader.

Emily: I love to read! I read all the time! Right now, I'm reading all the Ivy and Bean books, but I also love Jada Jones, Critter Corner, Heidi Heckelbeck, and Yasmin. Have you read those? My mom and I are reading all the Kate DiCamillo books at home. I am reorganizing all my books at home so that all my favorite series are together and in order.

Jen: What do you think about when you pick books?

Emily: When I find a character I like, I read every book in the series.

Jen: So, right now, you're the kind of reader who really falls in love with characters and with series books. That happens to me, too.

Throughout the conference, Jen listened with care and asked follow-up questions as needed. Jen invited Emily to share some insight into her reading life with two process-oriented questions: "Tell me about yourself as a reader" and "What do you think about when you pick books?" The student eagerly shared her preferences and habits, indicating a strong positive attitude and sense of self-efficacy. Jen chose to provide strengths-based feedback related to book choice, as this was a habit she wanted to encourage that student to continue and build upon.

Later in this same conference, Emily read aloud from and talked about one of her favorite parts of her current independent reading book. She read with confidence and was able to share well-developed inferences into the character and plot.

Afterward, Jen reflected on the conference and looked at other small data. Looking at Emily's book logs, Jen realized that Emily regularly selected similar kinds of character-driven series, most of which were realistic fiction or animal fiction. She wondered how to expand the student's identity to try on a series from another genre.

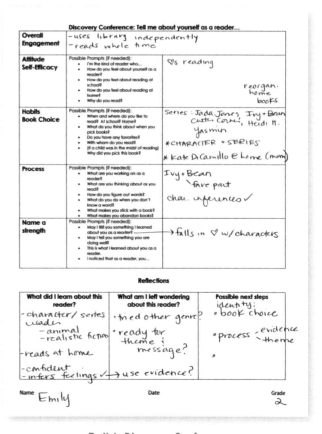

Emily's Discovery Conference

Jen also looked at a recent benchmark assessment and notes from class read-aloud discussions. She noted Emily's ability to think and talk about characters and hypothesized that further impactful work could include how to consider theme and message. Going into the Intention Conference, Jen planned to listen to Emily's thoughts about her work as a reader with these various possibilities for future instruction in mind.

Scenario Two: Davon's Story

In this conference, Hannah worked with Davon, an easygoing fourth-grade student who was not a frequent contributor to whole-class discussions but talked more easily in small groups. Through kidwatching, Hannah already knew that Davon tended to get started with independent reading right away, tried on the work of the minilesson, and read for the entire independent reading block.

Hannah: Tell me about yourself as a reader.

Davon: I like reading? I'm not really sure what you mean.

Hannah: Let me tell you what I mean. You could talk about what you like to read or where you like to read, or tell me some favorite books.

Davon: Ohhh. I like reading mysteries. [*Silence.*]

Hannah: Could you take me on a tour of your book stack? How did you pick these books?

Davon: Well, I got this from the mystery basket because I love mysteries. I have this graphic novel that my friend gave me. And then I grabbed this book about camping because my family is going camping this summer.

Hannah: May I share something I just learned about you as a reader? Right now, you're the kind of reader who picks their reading with a strong reason in mind. As a result, you have a lot of very different reading in your stack!

With Davon, Hannah used process-oriented questions and a tour of his current book selections to gain more insight into Davon's reading identity. At the start of the conference, you will notice Davon seemed unsure of how to talk about himself as a reader. This is not atypical; many students are unsure of how to answer this question when encountering it for the first time. Students may not be used to talking about their reading lives in this way and so Hannah gave a bit more explanation to support Davon's thinking. Ultimately, this bit of nonjudgmental support unlocked Davon's ability to share information about himself as a reader, and Hannah was able to end the conference by providing strengths-based feedback in which she named the student's clear purposes for selecting a range of reading material.

After the conference, Hannah took out Davon's recent informal running records, noticed that Davon typically shared a surface-level understanding of his reading, and hypothesized that moving beyond literal comprehension would be beneficial work. She also looked more closely at small data related to gauging talk and wondered how she might support Davon to share his ideas with the larger class community.

Finally, Hannah realized that this was the sixth student who needed support to begin talking about themselves as a reader, and she decided to address this with the class later, as an entry point into a short inquiry into what it means to talk about yourself as a reader.

Discovery Conference: Tell me about yourself as a reader...		
Overall Engagement	Transfers strategy from mini-lesson to his own reading Reads for all of I.R. Talks to reading partner	
Attitude Self-Efficacy	Possible Prompts (if needed): • I'm the kind of reader who... • How do you feel about yourself as a reader? • How do you feel about reading at school? • How do you feel about reading at home? • Why do you read?	"I'm not sure what you mean." "I like it."
Habits Book Choice	Possible Prompts (if needed): • When and where do you like to read? At school? Home? • What do you think about when you pick books? • Do you have any favorites? • With whom do you read? • (If a child was in the midst of reading) Why did you pick this book?	"I like it to be quiet." "I like mysteries." – graphic novel - from a friend – camping book - family trip
Process	Possible Prompts (if needed): • What are you working on as a reader? • What are you thinking about as you read? • How do you figure out words? • What do you do when you don't know a word? • What makes you stick with a book? • What makes you abandon books?	"Just reading." Trying to figure out who the thief is. "I can read a lot of words."
Name a strength	Possible Prompts (if needed): • May I tell you something I learned about you as a reader? • May I tell you something you are doing well? • This is what I learned about you as a reader. • I noticed that as a reader, you...	• You make purposeful book choices. • You read a variety of books.

Reflections

What did I learn about this reader?	What am I left wondering about this reader?	Possible next steps
–likes different genres – likes solving the mystery – unsure of what it means to talk about himself as a reader	–What is his comprehension like? (check running records)	book talk → connect to similar reader strategies for different genres

Name Davon   Date   Grade 4

Davon's Discovery Conference

Scenario Three: Akiko's Story

Akiko, a third-grade student, was reluctant to talk about her reading, claiming to dislike it. Through small data collection aimed at gauging engagement, Jen had observed that Akiko often displayed visible signs of disengagement such as fidgeting and abandoning books. Jen approached the conference with curiosity, wanting to understand Akiko's reading identity, not problematize it.

Jen: Tell me about yourself as a reader.

Akiko: I don't like to read. I hate doing it.

Jen: Can you take me on a tour of the books you have here? How did you choose them?

Akiko: I just grabbed them. They're all boring.

Jen: Tell me about yourself as a reader outside of school.

Akiko: I still hate it.

Jen: What do you like to do?

Akiko: I just like to play with my dogs and play my video games.

Jen: You have dogs? I didn't know that. Can you tell me more about your dogs?

Akiko: My family fosters dogs. We always have a lot of dogs in the house and I help to take care of them.

Jen: Right now, you have important things that you care and know a lot about. That can be part of who you are as a reader too.

This conference presented Jen with a challenge with which we are all familiar; although this was a classroom that embraced choice and time for independent reading, this child in particular had not yet exhibited engaged behavior while reading. After asking a few process-oriented questions, Jen realized that time would be better spent working to connect with Akiko. By working to learn more about Akiko, Jen aimed to lay a more trusting foundation for future conferences and to gain insight into how she might use this information to create more positive reading experiences. Jen ended the conference by naming Akiko's strength: she is the kind of reader who has topics about which she cares.

Following the conference, Jen reflected on other conversations and book logs, noting that Akiko did not seem to have any clear reading preferences. Recent informal running records revealed that Akiko had transferred some instruction to independence, as she used several decoding strategies and was able to summarize her reading. However, Jen noted that the connection to reading was still absent in these contexts as well. She hypothesized that working to find a topic, genre, or author that connected to Akiko's life might help create more interest.

Reading Identity and Engagement

Akiko's Discovery Conference

Understanding all aspects of students' identities as readers is a key factor in creating experiences that intentionally invite engagement. The better you know your students as readers, the better able you are to craft instruction that invites engagement. To be clear, engagement is not a separate aspect of reading identity; rather, a student's level of engagement shapes how their identity might evidence itself on any given day. Think of engagement as an umbrella that overarches the work and identity of readers. For example, picture a highly engaged reader who chooses books independently and with purpose, prefers fiction over nonfiction, and often gets lost in books or consumed by self-selected author studies. This same reader, when directed to read nonfiction, will often have a hard time focusing and struggle to transfer previously taught strategies with independence. The same reader can live in different places on the Reading Engagement Continuum depending on the invitations that are extended to them each day.

While engagement can help to explain how a reader's sense of identity is enacted, it can also be the key to figuring out how to better engage readers. For example, when a student consistently exhibits signs of disengagement or compliance while reading, a first step is to consider reading identity. Similarly, an engaged reader might present a puzzle for the teacher because next steps might be less obvious. The following are some examples of a range of reading behaviors from the Reading Engagement Continuum (Online Resource 3.1) and the questions related to reading identity that teachers might ask themselves in order to provide tailored feedback.

Digging Deeper into the Reading Engagement Continuum	
Disengaged Behavior	**Questions Teachers Might Ask Themselves**
A student consistently abandons books.	How can we grow a better idea of what readers think about when they choose books? How might expanding *book choice* support this student?
A student consistently finds a variety of reasons to not engage with text.	How does this student choose books? Does the library include book selections that represent the student's interests, experiences, background, and so on? How does this student feel about themselves as a reader? What is this student's attitude toward reading? Have they had enough positive reading experiences?
A student exhibits clear frustration with a text (or texts) that results in disengaged behavior.	What strategies can the student call upon with independence? What strategies might be needed to better support this reader? How does the reader work to reengage themselves?
Compliant Behavior	**Questions Teachers Might Ask Themselves**
A student reads the same book every day for an extended period of time.	How does this student choose books?
A student follows classroom routines but regularly reports being bored.	What does the student imagine as a purpose for reading?
A student regularly tries to do the work of the minilesson even when that work does not apply to their chosen text.	How can I bolster the student's sense of confidence as a decision maker?

continues

Engaged Behavior	Questions Teachers Might Ask Themselves
A student regularly begs to talk to you about books.	Can the student set up a book club?
A student likes to read every text available in a specific genre or series.	How can I use what I know about genre to expand this student's book choice?
A student is regularly moved or emotionally invested in their reading.	How can I bolster this student's sense of self-efficacy so that they feel able to share their thinking in ways that inspire others? What strategies can I use to inspire the student to critique their experience in various books?

Recognizing Implicit Bias and the Danger of Labels

When we work to get to know each child's story as a student and as a reader, it is essential to note the role implicit bias can play in the construction of these narratives. As we discussed in the introduction to Part 1, implicit biases are the assumptions and stereotypes we hold and the unintentional actions we make toward others based on identity labels. Because implicit biases are so deeply internalized, it means that we often act upon these biases without even realizing it or considering the impact these decisions might have.

In the school context, teachers' implicit biases can impact the ways in which they discuss and label children. For example, in data meetings, teachers might discuss students who are not making expected learning gains and refer to these students as "low readers," "strugglers," or "troublemakers." These kinds of labels serve only to narrow our vision of the child. They represent a deficit approach and focus on what students *can't* do, influencing how we think about them (Minor 2019). For example, bilingual students are often viewed as lacking or as less sophisticated speakers and interpreters of complex language practices than their native English-speaking peers (España and Herrera 2020). Ability labels such as these are highly correlated with teacher expectation of student performance (Howard, Milner-McCall, and Howard 2020). The problem is magnified when these sorts of labels are continuously associated with students from a particular identity group, such as boys, Black students, or children from lower socio-economic classes.

Research is clear on the devastating effects of having low expectations for students. According to a National Education Association report (2016), teacher expectations are one of the most impactful in-classroom factors on student achievement. This report finds that teachers expect less, on average, from Black students than white students. This sets off a dangerous cycle of low expectations and low performance. When we expect students to fail, the students are more likely to fail. This same report also acknowledges the power of positive student-teacher relationships. Committing to our own reflection and deep identity work is the only way to uncover, acknowledge, and begin to address our own implicit biases within the context of the systemic racism that shapes them. During the critical relationship building that takes place during conferring, we must pay attention to and disrupt these biases in order to open up spaces for children to define themselves.

Another example that is common shorthand among teachers is the label of "high reader" or "high flyer." These sorts of labels are dangerous in that they oversimplify the student and the act of reading, assuming that a voracious reader will never need support as they encounter increasingly complex text. As a result, these students are often given less time and attention because teachers assume they will progress on their own.

Finally, we need to take a broad view of literacy, as bias can also manifest itself in how we view texts and students' choices of texts, as well as their understanding of literacy. If we grimace slightly when the tenth student says, "I love graphic novels," we are inadvertently judging them, their choices, and all graphic novels. The same goes for students who like to read books we may not consider to be of high quality, such as books that are based on Disney movies. If we ask a child about reading at home, and the child tells us that Grandma tells them stories, we should honor that oral storytelling as an important tradition.

In order to move beyond these biases to create more equitable opportunities for all students, teachers can utilize the following strategies:

- *Acknowledge your bias.* Before educators engage in work alongside children, they must engage in their own self-work, taking the time to reflect upon and acknowledge their own experiences, assumptions, and biases (Muhammad 2020).

- *Slow down to get to know students.* Getting to know another person as fully and authentically as possible is not something that you can rush. Avoiding assumptions requires time to both listen with empathy and check your own biases (Eberhardt 2019).

- *Rely on your colleagues.* Call upon the power of collective teacher efficacy by checking in with other colleagues to get their point of view on a student or situation.

- *Connect with families.* Devote time to get to know the student's family or caregivers.

How the Discovery Conference Impacts Independent Reading

While the Discovery Conference reveals a great deal about a single student, listening *across* students can reveal patterns. By viewing these patterns as feedback, we can begin to recognize implications for independent reading for individuals as well as future whole-class reading work. The following chart offers a few examples of common patterns and some reflective questions that lead to teacher action. Noticing and naming these patterns allows teachers to make informed decisions about further instruction needed to support independent readers.

Sample Discoveries and Possible Next Steps		
Example Observation	**Reflection Questions**	**Possible Next Steps to Take with the Class**
While taking a tour of their book boxes, many students share that they consistently abandon books.	• What types of texts are the students able to manage with success? • How do these students currently select books? • How do these students perceive themselves as readers?	• Teach how to transfer successful reading habits across different text types or genres. • Teach into how to read and manage longer text selections. • Teach into how to select books with a variety of clear purposes or reasons in mind. • Partner these students with others who have similar reading tastes and ask them to talk about how they can navigate the text together.
When asked, "What are you thinking about as a reader?" many students answer by parroting familiar or current whole-class objectives.	• What do my students state and not state when asked, "What are you thinking about as a reader?" • What is the current level of engagement of these students? How do I know?	• Use the read-aloud as a springboard for naming students' thinking. Highlight that the students all heard the same book, and they all were thinking about different aspects of the book.

continues

Sample Discoveries and Possible Next Steps, *continued*

Example Observation	Reflection Questions	Possible Next Steps to Take with the Class
A group of students select only graphic novels (or another specific type of text) to read. Or A group of students read an overwhelming amount of nonfiction (or other genre).	• What if our class embraced this current preference? • How do these students currently select books? • How might I inspire these students to identify and then read into their gaps? • How can I use my students' love of one text type or genre to broaden their book choices?	• Conduct a class deep dive into graphic novels, comparing and contrasting various titles that rely on this art form. • Conduct an inquiry that compares and contrasts two text types (e.g., graphic novels and prose). • Conduct an inquiry into these students' book preferences. Challenge this group to read into their gaps and reflect together. • Engage students in short book talks that sell favorites to the rest of the class. Be sure to have extra copies on hand if possible.
A number of students give brief answers, despite follow-up questions and ample wait time.	• What is the class' definition of reading identity? • Have I provided enough examples or models of this sort of talk?	• Model talking about your own reading identity, noticing and naming the different aspects. • Encourage students to draw and write about their own reading identity, taking care to address multiple aspects. • Create a whole-class definition of *reading identity*. • Provide sentence starters such as "I like to read . . ." and "I feel good as a reader when I . . ."
Many students proclaim that they dislike reading.	• How can I create a wider variety of positive reading experiences? • Have these children ever experienced true engagement with a text? When? How?	• Observe the students' level of engagement during different components such as read-aloud, partner reading, shared reading, and independent reading. What are they doing or not doing? • Provide opportunities to engage in a wider variety of text types, such as visual texts, poems, and songs.

Give It a Go: Discovery Conferences

The Discovery Conference allows us to spend time with children in ways that honor vital parts of our teaching hearts. It provides space for us to gather a more complete picture of the child and sets us up to make instructional choices alongside children that are less likely to originate from assumptions or partial information. In the Discovery Conference we collect information that elevates the voice and identity of each child, adding these key insights to a wealth of data. We trust students to lead the way. In addition, the Discovery Conference allows us to build a relationship with each student centered on text and how reading can impact the way we come to know the world.

We encourage you to get started by trying this with just a few students. Take a moment to consider three students in your classroom or three students with whom you work, if you are a reading specialist who does not have your own classroom. Is there a student you wonder about? A student who baffles you? Or a student you just want to get to know better? Use the table in Online Resource 4.2, Give It a Go: Discovery Conferences (shown on page 98) to jot down what you already know about these three students as readers. Now, go and hold your own Discovery Conferences with them. Come back to the chart on page 98, and write what you know about these students as readers *now*. How did the Discovery Conference open up new spaces of possibility or expand what you already knew about each student's reading identity?

Date: _____ Grade: _____

Give It a Go: Discovery Conferences

Name	What do you know about this student as a reader already?	What did you learn about this student after a Discovery Conference?	What are reflection and teaching implications for the student?	What are implications for independent reading?

5

Trust Readers to Take the Lead

The Intention Conference

A conference is essentially an invitation to glimpse the intersection between a student and a text.

—Dorothy Barnhouse

Setting intentions allows students to take the lead in creating pathways for reading instruction that feel relevant to them, making this instruction more likely to transfer into independence. In this chapter, we outline the second conference in the Cycle of Conferring, the Intention Conference. In this conference, you devote time to uncovering students' authentic intention for meaning making in order to provide tailored feedback that is relevant to the students and invites deliberate practice. The Intention Conference positions students as equal experts in their reading growth, as they are the ones who possess the most expertise in naming what it is they truly want and hope to do as readers.

Marquis, an exuberant kindergartner, bounded into the classroom each morning and made a beeline to the basket of superhero books. He spent as much time as he could engrossed in these books, poring over the pictures and making up stories to go along with them. When he did this during independent reading, his level of engagement soared. Marquis' intention was to make meaning out of the books through the pictures and his prior knowledge of superhero stories. While Marquis' teacher wanted to honor his book choice, *her* intention was to support him in identifying letters and sounds and pick books that he could begin to decode. Although both are appropriate and well-reasoned intentions, the distance between the teacher's goal and Marquis' goal was huge and difficult to navigate. How could the teacher bridge this gap?

Marquis' teacher recognized the power of inviting engagement and valued his choices as a reader yet was determined to also support Marquis in his ability to identify sounds and letters. She gathered more superhero books for the classroom library, and during independent reading, she conferred with Marquis while he made meaning from these texts, providing feedback related to the elements of story readers can infer from the pictures. During the other components of balanced literacy, she focused on providing Marquis with direct instruction related to foundational skills. As his ability to decode improved, he started to add the books he read in small-group instruction and copies of shared reading texts into his book box. One day, during independent reading, Marquis was deeply engaged in a superhero book when he shouted: "Look! The pictures and the words go together in this book too! This says, 'He ran'!"

> While we trust our students to take the lead, we trust ourselves to find spaces of possibility within that work to grow our students as readers.

When we checked on Marquis at the end of the year, he was reading on grade level and still an avid reader of all things superhero. By valuing time, choice, and her ability to provide teacher support in a variety of ways throughout the school day, Marquis' teacher was able to bridge the gap between Marquis' intentions as a reader and her intentions for him as a learner. She honored his intentions for reading while providing critical foundational instruction, which resulted in a powerful moment of transfer and, ultimately, increased reading success.

Students enter our classrooms already living their reading lives. Our role is to nurture their reading identities by making space for them to continue and expand upon the types of meaning making that fuel their desire to read. The Intention Conference bridges the distance between students' authentic ways of making meaning and the learning experiences our expertise tells us they need in order to grow as readers. We position students' ways of meaning making as the entry point for instruction, sending a clear message that we recognize their ability to be agentive readers. While we trust our students to take the lead, we trust *ourselves* to find spaces of possibility within that work to grow our students as readers. When we prioritize and honor student-driven work, we can design instruction that is relevant to the reading lives of students.

Reading Intentions

Supporting students' ability to set and pursue their own goals and intentions for reading has been shown to not only increase motivation but also lead to improved performance, impact levels of effort, reenergize students, and have a positive effect on persistence (Förster and Souvignier 2014; McTigue, Washburn, and Liew 2009; Locke and Latham 2006, Schunk 2003). Both choice and relevance are strong motivators (Fisher, Frey, and Quaglia 2018) that can buoy student and teacher engagement and willingness to persevere. Encouraging students to choose their own intentions for meaning making is a powerful, deliberate act that is rooted in a strong belief in both agency and independence, which are central to our work and are hallmarks of the most successful reading classrooms.

An intention refers to what a person *plans to bring about*; within the reading classroom, we define an intention as the plan a reader makes for actively constructing meaning from text. When students set an intention for reading, they name a self-selected purpose for reading or a way to make meaning that feels relevant to *them*. Intention setting ensures that we support students to set goals from their perspective and in their own language. It highlights reading identity and the work *students* believe to be most important to their reading lives. Intention setting positions students to be experts in what they want to pursue and teachers as experts identifying the literacy learning possible within that intention.

The Intention Conference: Following a Student's Lead

The Cycle of Conferring moves from the Discovery Conference to the Intention Conference. In the Intention Conference, students voice *their* intentions as readers and, with the support of the teacher, turn those intentions into plans. The Intention Conference is divided into three distinct sections. The first section of the conference asks students to reflect upon and explore how they naturally work to make meaning from text. In the second section of the conference, the student and teacher explore options for setting an intention for independent reading together. Finally, in the last section of the conference, the teacher clearly poses the student's intention as a what-if question and then names a strength the student already possesses in relation to their intention, setting them up to build upon this foundation.

Sharing learning intentions is a fundamental requirement for both learning and feedback (Hattie and Clarke 2019), but it may not come naturally to all students without

The Intention Conference

Notice and listen

What are you doing as a reader?

Explore options
Name the intention

What are you thinking about as you read?

What do you want to do as a reader?

What if . . .?

How might you get started?

Sketch a plan

What questions do you need to ask?

How might you share this with others?

Give strengths-based feedback

May I tell you why this feels right for you?

support. In the Intention Conference, we keep the talk grounded in the student's own language by framing the intention as a what-if question. These student-driven intentions turned into what-if inquiries harness the power of the question in that they are open-ended, thought-provoking, and recur over time. Further, they spur additional questions and call for higher-order thinking, all qualities of a robust essential question (Wiggins and McTighe 2013) that has the potential to compel transferable thinking that will increase the proficiency of each reader.

In the Intention Conference, we respect all student intentions as valid and full of possibility. Some students might say they "want to learn how to read more words" while others may decide they want to learn everything there is to know about leopards. When we trust children to do what they feel inspired to do as readers, offering them freedom to make decisions about their reading time and efforts, we strengthen their reading identities. We trust ourselves as teachers to imagine how to find space inside this work to build in natural connections to key skills and strategies.

In our work with students, we have found that there are three common entry points to students' intentions for meaning making:

- *Reading identity:* self-efficacy, attitude, habits, and book choice (reading process).
- *Reading process:* strategies required to flexibly solve words, read fluently, and comprehend text deeply
- *Community building:* authentic, purposeful talk or writing about the text

Think of these entry points as *how* students typically conceive of framing what it is *they* want to do as they approach reading. When listening to a student during the Intention Conference, you can ascertain the entry point that feels most relevant to the student's current independent reading work. The following is a chart that outlines these three entry points.

Framing What-if Questions		
Student's Entry Point for Establishing an Intention	What the Student Might Say	Possible What-if Question
Reading identity	• "I want to read information books about trucks." • "I love reading graphic novels." • "I like reading books that are about kids like me."	• "What if you spent some time reading all about trucks?" • "What if you immersed yourself in graphic novels?" • "What if we found new books and you built a collection of books that you relate to?"
Reading process: word solving, fluency, and comprehension	• "I'm thinking about the words." • "I like it when books connect." • "I get confused in long books."	• "What if we named some of the ways readers think about words together?" • "What if you created a collection of books that connected in some way?" • "What if we studied different ways to keep track of the text?"

continues

Framing What-if Questions, *continued*		
Student's Entry Point for Establishing an Intention	**What the Student Might Say**	**Possible What-if Question**
Community building	• "I want to start an adventure book club." • "I want to recommend my book to a friend." • "I want to write my own fantasy."	• "What if you started an adventure book club?" • "What if we matched some books to your friends for recommendations?" • "What if you used a fantasy you have read as inspiration for your own?"

When students frame their own intentions, they may not use academic language; however, that does not mean their intentions are not valid entry points that can lead to beneficial work. Throughout the Intention Conference, you can use your understanding of these student-driven categories to probe further in order to move beyond students' conceptions of what they are *supposed* to be doing and toward what they desire to do as readers. Online Resource 5.1, Intention Conference Template, is a template for you to use to take notes during the Intention Conference; it's shown in the following chart on page 105.

The Intention Conference is a conversation that lasts five to ten minutes with each child. Here are some tips to make the conference go smoothly:

- *Be prepared.* Have your Discovery Conference notes and reflections with you in order to tailor your feedback and questioning. Your notes remind you to center the story of each student. Make sure to have sticky notes, the Intention Conference Template, and your favorite pen ready to use.

- *Accept all student intentions without judgment.* Check your biases. The work that feels right to students is often related to their authentic purpose for reading. It is highly personal; sharing these thoughts might feel like a big risk for some students. Trust yourself to find standards-based, appropriate skills and strategies to embed into your support.

- *Listen and provide wait time.* Students will often start by sharing intentions that closely mirror what they believe it is we want them to do as readers. Give students the space they need to express their authentic intentions.

Name: _____ Date: _____ Grade: _____

	Intention Conference Template	
Overall engagement		
Notice and listen	What are you working on as a reader?	
Explore options	What do you think about when you read? What do you want to do as a reader? *Possible prompts (if needed):* • May I give you some suggestions? • I learned that you _____, so maybe you want to _____. • What do you find challenging?	
Name the intention	*Restate the student's intention in the form of a what-if question: What if you [name student intention]?*	
Sketch a plan	How might we get started? What are some of the questions you might have to answer? How might you share this with others?	
Give strengths-based feedback	May I tell you why I think this work makes sense for you?	
Reflections		
Possibilities for identity work	Possibilities for the reading process	Possibilities for talk and response

- *Probe for further information if needed.* Some students will simply shrug or share that they dislike reading. Prior to the Intention Conference, you may also want to take a moment to prepare one intention for each entry point that feels right for the particular child in case they need suggestions to get their thinking going.

- *Take notes as you go or make a recording.* The student's exact words are important, so jot down key phrases. Take a moment immediately after the conference to brainstorm possibilities for supporting future work.

The Cycle of Conferring repeats throughout the year, so you will return to setting intentions alongside students several times. Each time, in addition to taking your own conferring notes, you give the student a What-if Question Form. The student keeps the What-if Question Form to refer to during independent reading. Both teacher and students benefit when the student has this individualized reminder. Students are nudged toward focusing on their intention independently and have concrete reminders of the strategies or ideas from previous conferences. As a result, teachers can rest assured that students have the tools they need to get started right away.

On the lower grades form (page107), at the end of each Impact Conference, you or the student write or draw a strategy together in each box. On the upper grades form (page 108), the student may write the strategies in any way that makes sense to them, using sentences, bullet points, or visuals. There is also a space to record the student's contribution to the class; this does not need to be filled out right away. The idea for a contribution should, in fact, grow organically out of your upcoming Impact Conferences. Think about this line as a placeholder for how the students will share their learning with the larger classroom community. We will discuss contributions in more detail in Chapter 6. Refer to Online Resource 5.2, What-if Question Form for Lower Grades, and Online Resource 5.3, What-if Question Form for Upper Grades, for reproducible templates (shown on pages 107 and 108).

Supporting Students in Naming Intentions

When we put students in the role of expert in naming the work they want to do as readers, we cannot predict what they are going to say. Our job is to listen carefully, notice the instructional possibilities in what they are saying, and build on them. We know that sometimes, despite how much we value what children want to pursue as readers, the conference will not go smoothly. Page 109 offers a list of five teaching moves to help students uncover their natural entry point for meaning making or to nudge them into expanding their intention to be more appropriately challenging:

What-if Question Form for Lower Grades

What if _____

_____?

Contribution: _____

What-if Question Form for Upper Grades

What if _____

_____?

Contribution: _____

- *Invite challenge.* Readers can intend to make meaning from text by overcoming challenges they face as readers. Ask, "What do you find challenging as a reader?" Start by sharing your own challenges as a reader. This validates the fact that everyone has challenges, and it also positions challenges as possible intentions.

- *Create suggestions.* Inspire student intentions by crafting two or three suggestions that combine what you have learned about the student's reading identity with what small data has uncovered about the student's literacy learning. Using the entry points of identity, reading process, and community building as a guide, offer three personalized suggestions to pique a student's interest or inspire a student-crafted intention.

- *Connect the student with peers.* Inviting students to connect with other classmates who share a similar reading identity can aid in sparking or expanding student ideas. Instead of relying on you, the student can view other students as invaluable resources to inspire student-centered reading intentions.

- *Have the student self-reflect.* Asking students to pay more attention to their reading experience and then checking in later can be the push they need to identify reading needs or wants, thereby creating an entry point to intention setting.

- *Give personalized book talks.* Matching readers to books you think they will love has a tremendous impact on boosting student engagement and sparking an entry point for meaning making. Bring along two or three new selections that you handpicked for that student, using all that you have uncovered about the student thus far as a guide. Trust the power of the right book for the right child.

The Intention Conference in Action

The Intention Conference positions the student as an expert in their own reading life, including naming what it is they intend or need to do as readers. The conference sometimes involves bridging the gap between what a student needs or wants and a teacher's goal. Sometimes, students and teachers have the same intentions.

Here we continue with three scenarios that illustrate the different ways an Intention Conference might unfold through the thoughtful use of the teaching moves described earlier. Following each scenario, we include insight into our reflection and preparation for the upcoming Impact Conferences.

Scenario One: Emily's Story Continued

Jen continued to work with Emily, who clearly named an intention for her reading, establishing building community as her current entry point for meaning making. Here is the notice-and-listen portion of the Intention Conference:

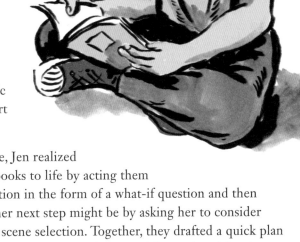

Jen: What do you want to work on as a reader?

Emily: I want to act out the books I'm reading. That would be so fun.

Jen: Tell me more about that.

Emily: Right now, I love, love, love the Jada Jones books.

Jen: I remember that. You are the kind of reader who falls in love with characters. What if you acted out your reading?

Emily: That would be so cool. Can I do that with my friends?

Jen: Sure! How would you decide which book to use or which part of the story to act out?

In this first part of the conference, Jen realized Emily's intention was to bring her books to life by acting them out. Jen revoiced Emily's own intention in the form of a what-if question and then prompted her to think about what her next step might be by asking her to consider book choice and the purpose of her scene selection. Together, they drafted a quick plan that consisted of questions Emily might consider as she moved forward with her intention (see page 111).

After the conference, Jen took time to outline several instructional possibilities that might arise within Emily's desired work. Jen noted Emily's intention was related to building community, so preparing for those possibilities first seemed natural. Jen then considered the two other common entry points, identity and the reading process, and prepared for those sorts of instructional possibilities as well (see page 111).

Jen would not have to cover all of these possibilities in the upcoming Impact Conferences. Rather, this outline represented possibilities so that she could prepare tailored instruction as she worked to follow this student's lead in later conferences.

What if I acted out my reading

Contribution: _____

think
What parts are worth acting out? Why?

Emily

9/2

Emily's What-if Planning Form

Preparing for Possibilities

What the student wants to do...	What we already know the student can do...	Possible Instruction Related to Identity	Possible Instruction Related to the reading process	Possible Instruction Related to Building Community
"act out favorite parts"	· reads fluently · literal compr · book choice: series	· How grow book choice to find new genre?	What parts of book inspire acting? why?	How can your scene inspire others' book choice?
			How does author develop char.?	What canvas can we have after?
			role of secondary character?	inspire writing?

Emily

Preparing for Possibilities with Emily

Scenario Two: Davon's Story Continued

In this second scenario, Hannah returned to work with Davon, a student who demonstrated a desire to read and a clear sense of reading identity during our discovery work. The following snippet shows how a conference might go when a student is unsure of their reading intentions. In this conference Hannah used the pathway of inviting challenge to uncover possibilities.

Hannah: What are you working on as a reader today?

Davon: I'm just reading.

Hannah: You seem really engaged in your reading today. What are you thinking about as a reader?

Davon: I don't know. I just kind of want to read.

Hannah: I understand. Remember when we had a discussion with the whole class about intentions? I am interested in what *you* feel is important reading work. Sometimes it helps to think about what is challenging. What do you find challenging?

Davon: Well, I do have a hard time keeping track of the story sometimes and feel lost, but I know I love the series, so I stick with it.

Hannah: So, what if we worked on ways of keeping track of the story? What do you already know about that?

In the first part of the conference, Hannah acknowledged that Davon's intention was to just read. The challenge in this conference was honoring Davon's intention while still opening up specific possibilities for student-driven reading growth. When considering how she might do this, Hannah returned to her reflections from the Discovery Conference and recalled that Davon was self-reflective and was apt to seek out help when needed. Therefore, the pathway of welcoming challenge to support intention setting worked for this reader (see below).

After the conference, Hannah took time to outline several instructional possibilities that could grow out of Davon's intention. Davon's intention was related to the reading process, so Hannah began her preparation by outlining those possibilities. Hannah then considered how Davon's intention might also lead to instructional possibilities related to identity and community (see below).

IDEAS FOR
WHAT IF QUESTIONS

· What if I collect the words that interest me?
· What if I compared one character to another?
· What if I figured out exactly what makes this book funny?

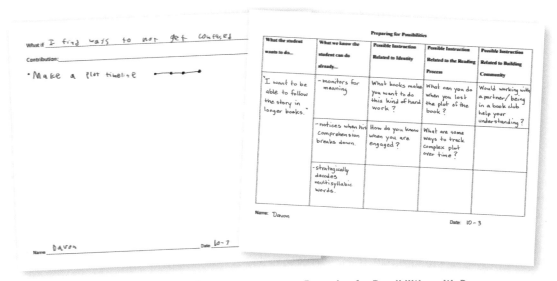

What if I find ways to not get confused

Contribution:

· Make a plot timeline

Name: Davon   Date: 10-7

Davon's What-if Planning Form

Preparing for Possibilities

What the student wants to do...	What we know the student can do already...	Possible Instruction Related to Identity	Possible Instruction Related to the Reading Process	Possible Instruction Related to Building Community
"I want to be able to follow the story in longer books."	- monitors for meaning	What books make you want to do this kind of hard work?	What can you do when you lost the plot of the book?	Would working with a partner/being in a book club help your understanding?
	- notices when his comprehension breaks down.	How do you know when you are engaged?	What are some ways to track complex plot over time?	
	- strategically decodes multisyllabic words.			

Name: Davon   Date: 10-3

Preparing for Possibilities with Davon

Scenario Three: Akiko's Story Continued

In this scenario, Jen continued her work with Akiko, who currently displayed disengaged behaviors. This snippet shows how we can connect with students by sharing a curated collection of books.

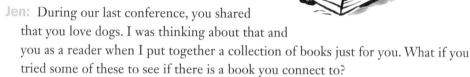

Jen: How's your reading going today?

Akiko: Blah. I don't really like to read.

Jen: Why don't you tell me how you chose these books?

Akiko: I just grabbed them. I don't really care about them.

Jen: During our last conference, you shared that you love dogs. I was thinking about that and you as a reader when I put together a collection of books just for you. What if you tried some of these to see if there is a book you connect to?

Akiko: Really? Sure.

Keeping in mind the belief that engagement is not fixed, Jen began the conference by asking Akiko about her reading work on that day. Realizing that Akiko had yet to engage with her reading, Jen shifted to connect with the student. Based on what she learned during Discovery, Jen came to the conference with a stack of books that were related to a topic important to Akiko. The books spanned fiction and nonfiction and, based on various small data sources, were within a range of complexity that would be comfortable for her. By giving brief book introductions, Jen set Akiko up to explore these texts (see page 114).

After the conference, Jen took time to outline several instructional possibilities that could grow out of Akiko's work to engage meaningfully with text. Akiko's intention was related to identity, so Jen began her preparation by outlining those possibilities. Jen then considered how once Akiko found texts she wanted to read, their work together might also lead to instructional possibilities related to reading process and community (see page 114).

Reflecting on Student Intentions: Identifying Instructional Possibilities

Teacher reflection and preparation after the Intention Conference is the bridge to the final conference, the Impact Conference. This reflection allows you to synthesize what you have learned about the reader thus far with your expertise in literacy learning to

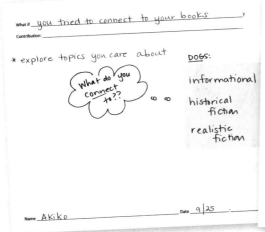

What if _you tried to connect to your books_ ?
Contribution: _____

* explore topics you care about   DOGS:

What do you connect to??

informational

historical fiction

realistic fiction

Name _Akiko_   Date _9/25_

Akiko's What-if Planning Form

Preparing for Possibilities

What the student wants to do...	What we already know the student can do...	Possible Instruction Related to Identity	Possible Instruction Related to the reading process	Possible Instruction Related to Building Community
"reading is boring"	· name interests · decode · read fluently when asked	—using interests to pick books —try different types of texts — which enjoy? —which book connect to?	how reading grows knowledge about topic? —compare/ contrast	—who shares interests? (read together?) —reading around interest inspire writing?

AKIKO

Preparing for Possibilities with Akiko

prepare for instructional possibilities within the student's intention. Thinking about how all three entry points relate to a student-named intention broadens the scope of instructional possibilities and allows you to be better prepared to follow a student's lead.

As you prepare to build a robust set of instructional possibilities tailored to the needs of each student, you can use the following reflection questions and a template to record student possibilities, like Online Resource 5.4, Preparing for Possibilities Template. Here are some reflection questions to keep in mind:

- How is this student entering the work of meaning making?
  - What strengths does the student possess within each entry point?
    - How might I use or build upon an aspect of their reading identity to support this work?
    - What comes next for this student in the reading process?
    - How might I use community building to support or expand the possibilities in this work?

As you continue to have additional Impact Conferences with a student, use this reflection and preparation work to ensure that your conferring both honors the student's intentions and grows their capacity as a reader. To be clear, you may not follow up on each of the possibilities you prepared for in the Impact Conference; rather, it is about being prepared to follow a student's lead in ways that are supportive and effective instructionally. Time spent preparing is never time wasted. This thoughtful work will allow you to not only better understand each student individually but also reflect on patterns across the class that might inform small-group or whole-class instruction.

Seeing Possibilities in Student-Named Intentions

What the Student Says	What We Might *Want* to Say	What We Can *Choose* to Do Instead
"I want to be able to follow the story in longer books."	"So your goal is to be able to recount key details in the story in order to determine the larger message."	• Talk about book choice and how it helps you stick with a book through challenge. • Prepare to teach one or two strategies for following the plot across a longer book. • Talk about paying attention to notice when you have lost track of the plot. • Partner this student with a student who has similar tastes in reading. Teach how partners can help each other.

Our teacher brains are wired to take a student's words and turn them into more formal, "teachery" goals that may get us away from the student's original intent. The above chart provides an example using Davon, the student from scenario two, who shared that he sometimes had trouble following the plot. In the first column, we highlight the student's intentions in his own words. In the second column, we give an example of what our teacher brain sometimes leads us to do when we try to take over a student's intention to make it fit the curriculum for the student. In the third column, we highlight the instruction that becomes possible when we unpack a student's intention as it is.

As you can see, when we resist the urge to translate a student's intention into teacher talk, we are able to come up with a varied range of possibilities and, therefore, are better prepared to follow a student's lead moving forward.

Independent Reading as Joyful Meaning Making

Reading is a joyful meaning-making activity; it is a transaction between the reader and the text (Rosenblatt 1978). When students consider *why* they are reading, all instruction related to that purpose suddenly becomes more relevant and transfer to independence becomes more likely.

When we open up choice and time for students to name how they enter the work of meaning making through the Intention Conference, we naturally invite increased engagement into independent reading. And when teacher support is inspired by student intentions, our instruction grows exponentially more relevant to students, increasing the likelihood of the transference of taught skills and strategies to independence.

Give It a Go: Intention Conferences

The Intention Conference allows us to bridge the gap between our curricular goals and students' personal intentions to make meaning as readers. It provides space for us to value this student-centered work while still imagining rigorous instructional possibilities related to all aspects of meaning making. In the Intention Conference we trust the student to lead the way and trust ourselves to have the expertise to follow with impactful teaching.

Think about the students with whom you tried the Discovery Conference. We encourage you to continue your work with these same few students. Begin by using the table in Online Resource 5.5, Give It a Go: Intention Conferences (shown on page 117) to jot down what you have learned about these readers as a result of discovery. Now, go and hold your own Intention Conferences with them. Come back to this table and write what you know about these students as readers and their intentions for reading *now*. How did the Intention Conferences open up new spaces of possibility for relevant and tailored teacher support?

Date: _____ Grade: _____

Give It a Go: Intention Conferences

Name	What do you already know about this student as a reader (from Discovery)?	What intention did the student name?	What are possible instructional next steps related to identity?	What are possible instructional next steps related to the reading process?	What are possible instructional next steps related to reading response?

Trust Readers to Do the Work

The Impact Conference

Our teaching superpower is listening . . .
listening will give us our children back.

—Cornelius Minor

Conferring allows teachers to provide impactful in-the-moment feedback to students as they pursue their unique reading what-if questions. This chapter addresses the Impact Conference, during which you devote time to supporting a student's intention by collaborating on an actionable plan and providing tailored instructional feedback. For the teacher, the guesswork of the conference is removed; prior to the conference, you outline possibilities for supporting student meaning making, placing both the student and their intentions in the center of your preparation. For the student, the conference is flexible and responsive; it provides relevant feedback that stems from your plans while letting the student take the lead in their reading life.

When we first met fifth grader Ben, he was sitting on the rug with his head buried in a book. During the Discovery Conference, he told us that he was reading the fourth book of a popular fantasy series. "I started it because my friend is reading it. He talked a lot about it, so he got me reading it, and then we got this other friend reading it," Ben explained. We asked him what he thought about when he read the series. He looked thoughtful and said, "I don't think about anything. I just like to read. I like fantasy." And then he launched into an enthusiastic summary of the series. We made sure to end our conference with Ben by naming a strength: we told him that he was the kind of reader who takes book recommendations from friends and deepens his understanding by talking about his reading.

During our Intention Conference, Ben was still immersed in the same series. "I just want to read," he said. "I don't think about anything, really. I just like reading it."

Realizing Ben might benefit from additional support, we referred him to a recently constructed read-aloud anchor chart, on which students had jotted what they thought about during the read-aloud. We prompted him to use the chart, saying, "Have a look at this chart and consider some of the things you and your classmates were thinking about during our read-aloud. What about some of these ideas?"

Ben looked over the chart and then said, "I did cry when the main character died." This was a light bulb moment! When given time, choice, and support to share his thinking, Ben recognized his connection to the main character, and he went from thinking of himself as a reader who loved fantasy to realizing that he was a reader who loved compelling characters. In the Impact Conferences, we were able to follow Ben's lead to deepen his understanding of the fantasy genre and to support his work in connecting with characters across a variety of genres, thinking about character motivation, character change, and author's craft.

The Power of Questions

In the Impact Conference, we continue to uncover our students' strengths related to their intentions by asking process-oriented questions, such as "How's it going with your reading?" and "What are you thinking about as a reader today?" Questions have an "unlocking effect" in people's minds and produce "a palpable feeling of discovery and new understanding" (Berger 2014, 17). By unlocking students' thinking, we ensure that we do not begin teaching too soon, cutting off natural paths of exploration and the creation of new understandings. We find that initiating the conference with broad questions opens up space for a wider range of responses that allow the teacher a glimpse into the student's otherwise invisible thinking.

Over the next few weeks, you will have several Impact Conferences with each student. Continue to rely on the power of questions to do in-the-moment research to find out what the students already know and might do naturally when faced with a meaning-making challenge. When we base instructional decisions upon this research, we can provide the right teaching at the right time.

Questions also have the power to transfer ownership of the learning to students. When we ask questions to explore students' thinking, we position them as experts who can make

Transferring Ownership of Learning to Students	
Instead of Stating This . . .	**Try Asking This . . .**
"Let's start learning about characters by . . ."	"What do you already know about how to get to know our characters?"
"You can find the meaning of that word by reading the sentences around the word for more context."	"What if we kept reading? Do you want to try it on your own or do it together?"
"Look all the way across to the final sound."	"What else could you try here?"
"Readers read with expression by thinking about how the character is feeling."	"What if you tried to read this in a story voice? How would that go?"

decisions about their own reading. Instead of saying, "This is what you do now," ask, "What if you tried this strategy now?" The above chart illustrates subtle changes in our language that shift ownership to students as they work to transfer other learning experiences into their independent reading work and build new understandings as they pursue their intentions.

The Impact Conference: Teaching into Intentions

After the Intention Conference, you prepared a list of instructional possibilities. During the Impact Conferences, which balance research and feedback, you'll turn these instructional possibilities into teaching points.

We translate the student's intention into skills and then strategies. Once we have determined the *skills* that will serve the reader, we can better prepare for the Impact Conferences by identifying the specific *strategies* that will most likely support the reader. Educators use the terms *skill* and *strategy* in different ways. Based on the work of Jennifer Serravallo (2015), we define them in the following way:

- A *skill* is the overarching term for what the reader is doing. Skills might be related to all aspects of reading identity, the reading process (including word solving, fluency, and comprehension), reading response, or engagement.

- A *strategy* is a step-by-step procedure that a reader can follow to accomplish a skill. Strategies will become automatic over time.

The Impact Conference has three distinct sections: notice, name, and next. During the first section of the conference (notice), the teacher prompts the student to reflect on what they are doing as a reader. Through observing, questioning, and listening, the teacher assesses in order to name a strength and to determine if the student is ready for a new teaching point. In the second section of the conference (name), the teacher provides strengths-based feedback that will serve the student well as they continue to pursue their intention. In the final section of the conference (next), the teacher provides feedback in one of two ways: by reiterating a strength or providing next steps. Online Resource 6.1, Impact Conference Template (shown on page 122), provides a form for taking notes during a single Impact Conference. Online Resource 6.2, Impact Conference Note-Taking Over Time Template, is a form for keeping notes on the Impact Conferences you hold over time with the same student. This is likely what you would use on a regular basis as it is informative to look at the work done over the course of several conferences.

The Impact Conference

Notice
How's it going with your "what-if" question?
What are you doing as a reader?

Name
May I give you a compliment?
You have been . . .

Keep going with . . .
A next step
for you is . . .
Next

Name: _____	Date: _____	Grade: _____

Impact Conference Template

What-if question	
Overall engagement	

Notice	How's it going with your what-if question? What are you working on as a reader? Last time we met, we talked about . . .	
Name (strengths-based feedback)	One of your strengths as a reader is . . . May I tell you something that you are doing well? I notice you . . .	
Next (next-steps feedback)	Keep going with . . . A next step for you is . . . What if we tried . . . ?	

Reflections

What Did I Learn about this reader?	What questions do I still have?	Possible next steps/ strategies

Ideas for Checking Back In	
Possible Time to Check in with a Student	**What It Sounds Like**
Five minutes after the conference	"How's it going with what we talked about?"
At the end of independent reading	"Please share with the class what you tried today."
At the start of the next day's independent reading	"Are you ready to keep going with the work from yesterday?"
When reading their reader's notebook	"Take a moment to jot how it is going today."
During partner work	"Today at partner time, talk about what new work you tried today."

We can end the conference by promising to be back soon to check in on how the work is going (Anderson 2018). The checking-back-in time is as important as the conference itself. When we hold ourselves accountable for checking back in with students, students are more likely to hold themselves accountable. Depending on how the student is doing, we can offer quick clarifications or encouragement.

The above chart illustrates different ways to check in briefly with each student after an Impact Conference.

The Impact Conference in Action

Each conference begins with researching what the student is working on using open-ended, process-oriented questions. As we listen to students' responses, reflection questions guide our decision-making and ensure that our feedback builds upon student strengths and evidence of the transfer of skills taught throughout the day into independent practice. The following chart helps to illustrate the flow of reflection and decision-making that occurs during the notice portion of the Impact Conference and that yields effective teaching decisions during this conference.

You can think of the process this way:

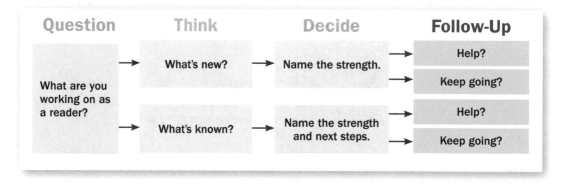

Question	In-the-Moment Reflection While Student Answers	Decision-Making	Follow-Up Question(s)
1. Ask: "What are you working on as a reader?" 2. Listen: What is the student doing with strength and independence?	Is this strength new? Will it serve the student as they pursue their intention?	I will name the strength for the student. I won't teach a new strategy today because my goal is to encourage the student to continue to transfer this strategy throughout their reading or to new texts.	"How might that help you moving forward?" "What are you going to do next?"
	Is this strength known? How can I build upon it in ways that will serve the student as they pursue their intention?	I will name the strength and then build on it by offering up a new strategy.	"What do you know about [name the skill]?" "What if we [name the strategy]?" "Do you want to give it a go on your own or together right now?"

A Flowchart of Teacher Decision-Making

In the following sections, we return to our work with Emily, Davon, and Akiko to illustrate how the Impact Conference might unfold.

Scenario One: Emily's Story Continued

In the Intention Conference, Emily quickly named a clear intention for making meaning: determining and acting out her favorite parts. In response, we revoiced this intention in the form of a what-if question, asking, "So, what if you acted out different parts of your reading?" and the student was off and running, energized with a new sense of agency and purpose. The following snippet came from our first Impact Conference with her.

Jen: What are you working on as a reader today?

Emily: I found a part I want to act out in my Jada Jones book. It's the part where she finally gives a speech in front of the whole school.

Jen: Sounds exciting! Tell me why you picked that part.

Emily: This is the part where Jada stops being afraid and talks in the auditorium. I have been waiting for this through the whole book!

Jen: It sounds as if this is an important change of feelings for the character. One thing readers do is pay attention to the moments when a character changes. What do you know about Jada's change?

Emily: She goes from being scared to not being scared of speaking.

Jen: How do you know?

Emily: I just know.

Jen: One of your strengths as a reader is noticing where the character changes. That is going to be important information for you to use when you act out this scene. May I teach you something new we can try? We can figure out how characters are feeling by paying attention to what they say and what they do. Let's give this a go while I'm here. Do you want to give that a try on your own or try it together?

Emily: Together.

Jen began with, "What are you working on as a reader?" opening up the possibility for the student to take the lead. Once Emily indicated that she was paying attention to the main character, Jen probed further into Emily's understanding by asking several

What if <u>I acted out my reading</u> ?

Contribution: _____

💭 think BIG What parts are worth acting out? Why?	💭 think small How is the character feeling? ⬇ by Pay attention: Say : do ?	

Emily   9/25

Emily's Updated What-if Question Form

process-oriented questions, which revealed an opportunity for teaching additional strategies for understanding character. Jen connected the student's strength back to her original intention before building upon it with her teaching. This teaching was not new; rather, it was something the class had done collectively through multiple read-alouds. Therefore, you will notice that after naming the teaching point, Jen positioned Emily to decide if she felt more comfortable trying it on her own or with more teacher support.

Scenario Two: Davon's Story Continued

You will recall that in the Intention Conference, Davon and Hannah collaborated to identify an intention: "What if you find ways to keep track of the stories you love?" The following snippet comes from the first Impact Conference with him.

Hannah: How's it going with your what-if question?

Davon: I'm using what we did in our read-aloud when we tried to keep track of what happens. Here is the plot timeline I started. But then there are too many characters and too many events and the timeline got messy, so I stopped.

Hannah: I want to tell you something you just did as a reader. You took something we worked on together as a class in our read-aloud, realized it might help you, and then tried it on your own! That shows how independent you are. You kept track of the plot by using a timeline.

Davon: Thanks . . .

Hannah: Would you like to talk through the timeline together or try a different strategy?

Davon: Can we do it together?

Hannah: Sure. Let's start by thinking about what was going well with your time line.

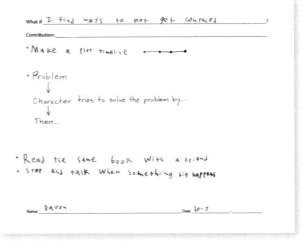

Davon's Updated What-if Question Form

Hannah began by researching how Davon had set about working toward his intention and uncovered that he had tried to transfer a strategy learned during a recent class read-aloud into his own independent reading. Hannah recognized this transfer work as a new strength and provided Davon with strengths-based feedback that clearly highlighted this. Continuing to follow the student's lead and grounding their work in Davon's intention, Hannah asked if he wanted to continue his work with this strategy or try on another way to keep track of complex plots. You will note that once Davon decided to keep going with his timeline work, Hannah began their collaboration from an asset-minded stance by asking Davon to reflect on his strengths with the use of this strategy.

See above, where Hannah and the student memorialized their collaborative exploration of plot timelines. By working alongside the student, Hannah was able to uncover key misunderstandings and provide meaningful next-steps feedback. This visible record of their work served to set up more deliberate future practice.

Scenario Three: Akiko's Story Continued

In both the Discovery and Intention Conferences, Jen learned that Akiko had yet to find engaging reading material. After working to connect with Akiko over her love of dogs, Jen offered her a curated book stack to invite more engagement with the intention "What if you explored some new books about a topic you love and paid attention to your thoughts and feelings about them?" The following snippet comes from the first Impact Conference; Jen observed that Akiko was flipping through the books and also had one opened in front of her.

Jen: How's it going with the new books?

Akiko: I'm looking at them. This one is OK.

Jen: Tell me more about that.

Akiko: It's about dogs and how they are related to wolves, which is cool. There are lots of cool pictures and photographs.

Jen: Is there a part you were really surprised by or interested in?

Akiko: This one. The photographs are real, not like the graphic novels everyone is reading. I don't get why they are the cool thing to read.

Jen: May I tell you something you do well as a reader? You have clear opinions about what you want to read. For you, what you like to read and your interests are more important than what is popular. Choosing books with this knowledge about yourself in mind is powerful. Are you planning on sticking with this book or looking for more?

Akiko: I want to find a few more so I don't get tired of this one.

Jen: Would you like a suggestion? *[Akiko nodded.]* Charlie is very into the same sort of information books you are. Another way you can find books you love is by connecting with people who have a similar reading identity and talking about your choices. Do you want me to help start that conversation, or do you want to do it on your own?

Akiko: I can do it on my own.

In this conference, Jen began by asking Akiko to share her thoughts about her book exploration. Once Akiko expressed an interest in the informational text, it was tempting to shift into teaching related to the reading process and discuss strategies related to digging deeply into the visual features of informational text. Yet the larger goal of Akiko's what-if question was to find more engaging reading material, so that ultimately the transfer of any specific skills and strategies taught would be more likely. Using Akiko's intention to ground the conversation, Jen took the time to follow Akiko's lead and continued to discuss book choice, working to uncover more about why that text felt more engaging than others. As a result, Akiko had the space to share self-reflections that revealed an important insight into her emerging reading identity. This was a reader who currently preferred nonfiction reading about certain topics but was also acutely aware of the popular preferences of other readers.

Jen provided Akiko with strengths-based feedback related to this key identity work and then offered suggestions for next steps that might serve to support

Akiko's emerging interest in informational text. After the conference, Jen revised her preparation to include the idea of researching how the student already made meaning from visual features or connected that information to what was in the print.

In framing conferences as opportunities to both research and provide feedback to students, we can revise possibilities for subsequent conferences to reflect our new learning about the students. The scenarios here illustrate how teachers can find spaces for student and teacher intentions to live side by side in the classroom.

What if _you tried to connect to your books_ ?

Contribution: _____

• explore topics you care about

What do you connect to??

• found someone to share your reading with? ☺☺

DOGS: Rate it!

informational — 5
historical fiction — 3
realistic fiction — 2

Name _Akiko_   Date _9/25_

Akiko's Updated What-if Question Form

Trusting Feedback

Effective feedback flows from teacher to student and student to teacher. The teacher provides students with information about their strengths, areas for improvement, and suggestions for how to improve (Fisher, Frey, and Quaglia 2018). The student gives the teacher feedback throughout the conferring cycle about their identity, their thinking, and their intentions as a reader, trusting that the teacher will support these ideas, creating a feedback loop.

Trust plays a key role in the effectiveness of feedback. Feedback is most powerful when the receiver and the giver trust each other. Students are most open to accepting and acting on our feedback if they trust us. The time we devote to getting to know them as readers inside and outside of school, elevating their voices in the read-aloud, honoring their decisions about how to organize the classroom library, and truly listening to them results in our students internalizing the feedback we offer. Trust allows our teacher support during the conference to succeed and promotes the transference of skills and strategies into independence. Feedback is at the heart of our ability to nurture engaged, joyful, and proficient independent readers.

While we give students feedback in all three conferences, the Impact Conference is a unique opportunity to harness the power of student-driven intentions in order to provide relevant strengths-based feedback and next-steps feedback at the ideal time for students to use it immediately. Feedback thrives on in-the-moment opportunities to both guide and celebrate the thinking of students.

Teaching Students How to Receive Feedback

Accountability is a word you cannot escape in schools. Teachers feel accountable to standardized tests and, therefore, feel as if they have to hold their students accountable for reading tasks aligned with the standards, regardless of students' engagement. When we feel responsible for covering curriculum without considering the students sitting in front of us, our teaching becomes limited. In many instances, a coverage approach to curriculum leads to "sham" accountability (Wiggins 2013). Students fill out reading logs, complete T-charts, and write a certain number of sticky notes, without being authentically engaged in the act of reading or understanding the purpose behind these tools. Instead, we have the chance to look at our teaching as a radical act to push back against these pressures. When students are engaged in their work, the trappings of sham accountability are no longer necessary. Authentic accountability means that we trust the students to do what they set out to do, while they trust us to guide them in the right direction.

The power of relevant feedback is amplified when we take time to teach students directly about the purpose of feedback. However, one commonly missing piece is teaching students *how to receive* feedback (Hattie and Clarke 2019). At times, students may make it challenging for us to provide feedback by squirming or talking a lot so that we are unable to find space to respond. Some may equate feedback with criticism and become defensive. Feedback is not a red pen; when we are compassionate, nonjudgmental, and kind, students can receive feedback in that spirit.

We can better equip students to receive feedback by teaching the purpose of the conference as well as student and teacher roles within it. Through modeling and direct instruction, we can explain the two kinds of feedback they will hear from us and how they might incorporate feedback into their reading. Here are some tips for cultivating authentic accountability:

- Conduct a whole-class inquiry into the purpose and structure of conferences and feedback.

- Make expectations visible by collaborating on a classroom chart, as illusrated here.

In a conference...

Students	Teachers
Talk about your reading.	Ask questions and listen.
Share your thinking.	Jot notes.
Say what you're working on.	Name a strength.
Try something new.	Suggest a next step.

Teacher and Student Roles During a Conference

- Explicitly explain the two types of feedback you will use frequently.
- Through the read-aloud or shared reading, model the two types of feedback and how they can incorporate them into their reading moving forward.
- Create a schedule for consistent conferring that includes both the Impact Conference and regular check-ins with students.

Crafting Effective Feedback

Because of the potential instructional impact of feedback, there is a wide range of research that captures the qualities of effective feedback (Hattie and Clarke 2019; Goldberg 2016; Wiggins and McTighe 2013). We know that feedback needs to be crisp, clear, and specific so that students can quickly move to deliberately practice the skill or strategy named. Here is some advice to keep in mind as you craft both strengths-based and next-steps feedback alongside students:

- *Consider language:* Effective feedback is accurate and agentive, demonstrating trust in our students to take on a challenge. Phrases such as "You can . . ." and "What if you . . ." position feedback as actionable. Our feedback compels future deliberate practice; before we move on to the next conference, students should be clear about what comes next.
- *Consider transfer:* Effective feedback is transferable to each student's specific intention. Questions such as, "How can you use this _____?" encourage immediate transfer.
- *Consider time:* Effective feedback is consistent and routine, allowing children to receive feedback, act on it, and have teacher support in a short time frame.
- *Consider visibility:* Effective feedback is visible, helping to anchor and focus student independent reading. When we ask students to jot down or say back to us what they took away from our feedback, we create ways to quickly assess our clarity, invite engagement, and set up deliberate practice once we walk away.

Deciding on Feedback That Names Strengths

When we listen to students to determine their *strengths*, we use those strengths to determine what comes next. As strengths emerge, we can decide which one is the most impactful to name for the student by asking ourselves the following questions:

- Which strength is most helpful to forwarding this student's intention for meaning making?
  - Is this strength new or emerging?
  - Is this an established strength?

By selecting the strength that would most likely benefit the student moving forward, we are able to promote continued deliberate practice with that particular skill or strategy (see below).

From Strengths to Next Steps		
Student Strength	**Teacher Reflection Questions**	**Possible Teacher Action(s)**
Word-Solving	Is this an emerging strength that could use more practice?	• Coach into word-solving as needed. • Add on another word-solving strategy for the student to try.
	Is this a well-established strength that I can build off of?	• Teach into monitoring for meaning. • Move to a more complex level of text. • Teach into fluency. • Check in on comprehension.
Book choice	Is this an emerging strength that could use more practice?	• Recommend a new series. • Set up a partnership or book club. • Talk about how book choice grows student reading identity.
	Is this a well-established strength that I can build off of?	• Teach into strategies for learning about characters. • Teach into strategies for learning about a character across multiple books. • Teach into how to determine the theme or lesson of each text.

Delivering Strengths-Based Feedback

A teacher's ability to clearly name a student's strength is well established as a beneficial teaching tool (Johnston 2004). Naming a strength is not the same as giving praise, as clear differences exist between the language and the outcomes of praise and feedback that names a strength (Johnston 2012). When we use phrases like "I love that you . . ." or "I like the way that you . . . ," we are giving praise, not feedback. This kind of praise can undermine students' sense of agency and shift their motivation toward pleasing the teacher. When naming strengths, try saying, "I notice . . ." or "You did this . . ." This language not only clarifies what the student has done successfully but also helps to transfer this strength into a student's sense of reading identity and encourages the student to continue to rely upon this strength.

In order to make this feedback stand out for the student, offset it from the rest of the conference. Students can prepare themselves to receive what we are about to say as it is intended: something worth celebrating! We find that the simple question "May I tell you something you are doing well?" makes a world of difference. Not only does the reader sit up a little taller with a broad smile, but they are able to feel successful, internalizing this strength as another positive aspect of their identity as a reader. The following chart provides some examples that illustrate the difference between praise and feedback.

Praise Versus Strengths-Based Feedback	
Praise	**Feedback That Names a Strength**
I am so proud that you figured out that word!	I notice that you stopped when you got stuck on a word. You tried different ways of figuring it out until you found the way that made sense in the sentence.
I love the way that you thought about the theme of the book.	As you were reading, you kept track of the places when the character learned a lesson. You used the lessons that the character learned to determine the theme of the book.
Nice work reading nonfiction!	As a nonfiction reader, you are paying attention to the main idea of each section and then summarizing in your own words the most important information.

Deciding on Next-Steps Feedback During the Conference

When we name a next step for the student, we usually do it in the form of a strategy. Clear next-steps feedback includes the intention of the reader and names the skill the student is working toward as well as a strategy that can help them take that next step. For example: "One way of following the plot [student intention] is to keep track of the important events [the skill] by stopping at the end of each chapter and writing a sentence that summarizes the chapter [the strategy]." Once you are familiar with this format, crafting feedback becomes second nature.

The chart on pages 135–136 illustrates how a student's intention can encompass a variety of skills and related strategies, making feedback simultaneously relevant to the student as an agentive reader with their current strengths and opportunities for growth.

We can draw a straight line between the feedback we provide students, standards to guide learning, and the skills required for proficient reading at specific levels of text. Keep in mind, these charts are an example of how intentions, skills, and next-steps feedback in the form of strategies can relate to one another. There are, of course, a plethora of strategies that students can call upon to accomplish any one skill; to decide on a specific strategy, consider all that you know about the student. For a thorough list of these possibilities, refer to Jennifer Serravallo's book *The Reading Strategies Book* (2015).

When we model, we

- use a familiar text such as the class read-aloud, a shared reading, or the student's own book;

- show the student how the strategy would work; and

- think aloud about our process.

When we coach, we

- use the class read-aloud, a shared reading, or the student's current independent reading selection; and

- listen and provide prompting as needed.

Delivering Next-Steps Feedback

Once you have determined what it is your students can do and what can be a valuable next step in pursuit of their intention, decide on the best method to deliver this next-steps feedback. You can model the strategy or coach the student as they try to implement the strategy on their own. This decision is based on your knowledge of the student and whether or not this is a strategy entirely new to the student or something they have had some exposure to in other literacy experiences.

Connecting Intentions, Skills, and Strategies

Possible Student Intention	Related Skill(s)	Possible Next-Steps Feedback (Strategy)
What if I read a series from start to finish? Entry point: reading identity	Book choice	• "You can pick a series to stick with by trying out the first chapter or first book in a few series. Read the first chapter or book and think: 'How do I feel about this book? Do I want to read all of these?'" • "One way to pick a series is to ask classmates for recommendations."
	Comprehension: monitoring for meaning	• "One way to read a series is to track the plot for each book. You can do this by creating a timeline of important events in each book." • "One way to make sure you are keeping the big events in your mind is to stop and ask yourself at the end of each chapter, 'What was the big thing that happened?'"
	Comprehension: inferring	• "One way to compare books across a series is to ask yourself, 'What lesson did the main character learn in each book?'" • "One way to get ready to read the next book in a series is to take a moment to think about what you already know about the characters. What can you expect in this book?" • "Another way to read the next book in a series is to stop and think, 'What do I know about how this series works? What can I expect in the next book?'"
What if I think all about the words? Entry point: reading process	Word solving	Lower grades: • "One way to think about the words is to figure out the word by looking at the first letter and last letter." • "You can look closely at a word to see if there are any parts or chunks that you recognize." Upper grades: • "One way to think about the words is to figure out the word by looking for chunks you already know." • "You can use information from the rest of the sentence to help you determine what kind of word that might be."

continues

Possible Student Intention	Related Skill(s)	Possible Next-Steps Feedback (Strategy)
What if I think all about the words? Entry point: reading process	Comprehension: monitoring for meaning	Lower grades: • "One way to think about the words is to stop and ask yourself, 'Does that make sense?'" • "Stop on each page and use your own words to say what happened or what you learned." Upper grades: • "When you come to a word you haven't heard before, look for all the clues in the text. Check the picture. Reread what comes before the word. Read the sentences after the word. Put all the information together to figure out the meaning of the word."
What if I started my own book club? Entry point: building community	Book choice	• "You can think about the kind of book club you want. Here are some options: identity, author study, theme study, and books of your favorite genre." • "One way to make a book club is to ask yourself: 'What do I know about the readers in my class? What kind of book club would they want?'"
	Comprehension: inferring	• "Readers decide on their own purposes for reading. Each person in the club can share their purpose and evidence in the text that goes with it."
	Comprehension: reading response	• "Readers decide how they want to respond to a book." • "Readers talk and decide: 'What can we contribute to the class that shows the work of our book club?'"

As agentive learners, our students can also be valuable resources regarding this decision once we have clearly named the strategy. By asking judgment-free questions such as, "Do you want me to show you?" "Do you want to try it with me?" or "Do you want to give this a go on your own while I'm still here?" we can again allow our students to show us the way.

The following are some tips for success:

- *Be prepared.* Have handy a conferring tool kit that includes different levels of familiar text, sticky notes, and planning forms for each student.

- *Be responsive.* Take comfort in your preparation and trust yourself to be ready to follow the student's lead.

- *Be positive.* Accept approximations or attempts with the new strategy. Find the strengths within the approximation, acknowledge them, and build from there.

- *Be accountable.* Stick to your schedule or revise your schedule as needed.

- *Take notes.* There is no one perfect note-taking system. The best system is the one that works for you. For some popular choices, please see our online resources.

- *Set the student up for success.* Leave behind an artifact of your work with the student as a reminder to help focus the student during future independent reading. Artifacts created together are the most powerful.

Assessing Impact Through Student Contributions

When children are engaged in meaningful work, they naturally want to share. In a classroom that intentionally invites engagement, children share their work not because it is a requirement but because it benefits others in the classroom community (Keene 2018). To that end, each Cycle of Conferring concludes with a student-initiated contribution.

These contributions can take a variety of forms and are not intended to become time-consuming projects. For example, a student whose intent was "What if I knew how to figure out the big words?" spent independent reading time learning and trying decoding strategies with teacher support. He created a minichart for the class to use, and a few students asked for a copy of the chart to put in their book bags. In the process of creating and presenting the chart, the student self-assessed which strategies he found the most beneficial as well as determined that he was ready for a new what-if question. At the same time, the teacher was able to gauge his level of independence with those strategies and then follow up with a running record.

Contributions are an opportunity for children to share their ideas, and they are also a form of assessment. As teachers analyze the contribution, they gain insight into how students understand the use of specific skills and strategies as well as how they have grown in their own ability to make meaning from text. In thinking about how their work around a specific intention grew their ability to make meaning, students are able to self-assess the impact of their independent reading efforts.

Some students may feel a sense of completion after three or four conferences, and others will feel as if they want to continue working within this intention for longer stretches of time. There is no specific timeline here. As students begin to express that their work within a particular intention is coming to a close or no longer feels as urgent, we turn the conversation to reflect on how their experiences or new understandings might benefit others. The following questions are effective in guiding readers through this reflective work:

- How has your what-if question helped you as a reader?
- What do you know or what can you do now that you felt less sure of before?
- What strategies were the most helpful to you?
- Are there other readers in the classroom or the school who might benefit from hearing about your thinking?

Below we share the contributions of Emily, Davon, and Akiko.

Examples of Student Contributions		
Student	**Intention**	**Contribution**
Emily	What if I acted out parts of my reading?	With friends, Emily acted out the climax of a favorite series book, shared the lessons characters learned, and shared the strategies she used.
Davon	What if I find ways to not get confused by complex plots?	Davon created plot timelines for the main characters in one of his favorite books. He invited classmates to hear about his work with this strategy, sharing his struggles and successes.
Akiko	What if I tried to find a book that I wanted to read?	Akiko gave a book talk on her favorite work of nonfiction and shared how this reading shifted her identity as a reader.

Here are some common contributions:

- newly curated book basket for the class library
- bookmark of strategies around a specific skill
- personal process chart of how to use a specific strategy
- book recommendations
- book talk
- list (of lessons learned, new books to try, etc.)
- a piece of writing inspired by reading
- an informal presentation (on a topic or opinion)

In order to further assess the impact of your teaching and the student's progress, you may decide to collect additional data. A quick, informal running record, notes on a student's participation in class discussions, or snippets from a student's reading journal can round out your understanding of a student's new strengths and future instructional possibilities. However, these small data opportunities arise most naturally in the moment. There is no need to create or assign additional assessments to students, which separates assessments from instruction and feedback.

Implications for Independent Reading

As students pursue their own intentions, there are both visible and invisible implications for independent reading. Signs of engagement are visible around the classroom: some children are talking about their reading together; others are in corners of the classroom engrossed in their books; still others are creating authentic ways to make their thinking public. Students can clearly talk about their current thinking as readers. Teachers are working one-on-one or with partnerships, talking about the work of readers and sitting shoulder to shoulder with children. In addition, there is a more invisible sense of pride, joy, and willingness to take risks as readers stretch their ability to make meaning from text in ways that feel relevant to them.

Give It a Go: Impact Conferences

The Impact Conference allows us to provide beneficial feedback to students as they make meaning from text in ways that feel relevant to their reading lives in the moment, increasing the likelihood that this work will transition into independence. By encouraging deliberate practice with specific skills and strategies that supports, rather than controls, the work of students, we create more authentic accountability and assessment measures as well.

We encourage you to return to the students you selected. Take a moment and prepare; how might you use their intention for meaning making to create opportunities to promote the integration of specific skills and strategies? Then, try sitting alongside each student, letting them take the lead; craft feedback using your preparation as a guide and see how smoothly the conference goes. Use the chart in Online Resource 6.3, Give It a Go: Impact Conferences (shown on page 141), to take notes on your thinking.

Now that you have tried this successfully with three students, go ahead and try it with more students. You may wish to expand to confer with another handful of students or you may feel ready to give this a go with your entire class. Eventually, you will go through the Cycle of Conferring with everyone. How does the Cycle of Conferring open up new spaces of possibility for all of your students to take an active role in their own ready growth?

Date: _____

Give It a Go: Impact Conferences

Name	Intention	Exhibited Strengths	Strengths-Based Feedback	Next-Steps Feedback

7

Trusting Time

You Can Do a Lot in 180 Days

*Students will read if we give them the books, the time, and the
enthusiastic encouragement to do so. If we make them wait
for the one unit a year in which they are allowed to choose
their own books and become readers, they may never read
at all. To keep our students reading, we have to let them.*

—Donalyn Miller

Prioritizing Independent
Reading in Your Day

Independent reading is every student's right. It provides the ideal setting for the personalized one-on-one conferring that establishes the trusting relationships required for students to flourish. When crafting a daily schedule, prioritize what you value. Fostering trusting relationships and learning students' stories through independent reading with conferring are *worthy* uses of classroom time. When we use worthiness as a deciding factor in how we spend our time, we ensure that our instructional time with students reflects our values. We prioritize choice, student agency, and joyful student reading experiences. Teaching with worthiness in mind keeps decisions about time grounded in our values. Our students, their instructional needs, and the privilege that it is to work with children reside at the forefront of our minds.

We want to ensure that we use classroom time to teach into the needs of readers themselves, instead of covering a list of skills deemed to be grade-level appropriate. Using the Cycle of Conferring as the method of teacher support during independent reading ensures that students are engaging with appropriate standards, skills, and strategies in ways that are impactful. Through discovery, intention, and Impact Conferences, our practice remains centered on uncovering what students know and can do as readers, using their strengths as a foundation for future instruction. Against a backdrop of robust reading opportunities throughout the day, time spent addressing instruction in this personalized way for students makes our teaching more relevant, increasing the likelihood that students will transfer these skills and strategies into their independent practice.

While routine brings predictability for children, adhering rigidly to a specific daily schedule does not allow space for us to be responsive to students. Debbie Miller (2019) wisely points out that reading instruction does not have to go the same way every day. Independent reading is the daily routine students need. The needs of our students guide how we use remaining time. For example, the minilesson might be at the beginning of reading or in the middle. Some days, you might not do a minilesson to make room for extended partner talk. When teachers make these kinds of intentional decisions, both they and their students thrive.

Reading Inquiries to Boost Independent Reading

Applying an inquiry approach to aspects of reading instruction means that students are actively involved in coconstructing understanding of key aspects of reading. Inquiry approaches to instruction help students to acquire knowledge while prioritizing understanding, which ultimately leads to a deeper understanding of the word (Murdoch 2015). Inquiry can unfold in a variety of ways. A key concept in inquiry classrooms is that teachers are not positioned as experts, but rather as guides. Students collaborate to be creators of knowledge.

Sources of Inspiration for Inquiries

Whole-class reading inquiries do not need to be overly complicated. We suggest conducting a number of short, focused inquiries across the year. Page 144 lists three sources for possible inquiries:

- *Student-generated topics*: As you confer and kidwatch, be on the lookout for patterns that bubble up naturally, such as topics of interest or aspects of craft. Students may pose questions that spark the interest or curiosity of the entire class during read-aloud, shared reading, or throughout the day.

- *Typical classroom problems:* Over the course of the year, we can expect some bumps in the road, such as taking too long to get started or serial book abandonment. Turn these classroom problems into teaching possibilities through inquiries. After all, the definition of *problem* is "a question raised for inquiry" (Merriam-Webster 2019).

- *Topics that are essential to independent reading:* The teacher determines an essential topic. You can plan when in the school year to introduce this inquiry, keeping in mind the option to revisit the same inquiries again later in the year.

The following are ten inquiry possibilities that are essential to independent reading:

- What is a reading identity? What is my reading identity?
- What is engagement? What does it mean to be an engaged reader?
- What is the purpose of a reading conference?
- What is feedback? How do I give it? How do I receive it?
- What does it mean to have an intention as a reader? What does it mean to think about what I am doing as a reader?
- How can I contribute to the learning of my class? How can I use my expertise or new learning to help others? What are the different ways we can share our thinking about books?
- How does reading with a partner or book club help me as a reader? What are ways partners or book clubs work together?
- How can we organize or reorganize the classroom library?
- How can I expand my book choice?
- What does it mean to read critically?

Any of these can be repeated over the course of the year to reflect students' evolving understanding and identities. For example, "What is my reading identity?" can become "What is my reading identity now?" later in the year.

We suggest using these inquiries responsively, tackling them as needed or desired over the course of five to six instructional days. Trust yourself to decide when these make the most sense for your class. Some inquiries lend themselves to the beginning of the school year or are better served to infuse new energy into reading after a lengthy school break. Others seem to fit seamlessly between units of study.

We move through three phases in each inquiry: posing a question with reflection, exploration, and final reflection. The chart below defines each of these phases and provides examples of what it might sound like in the classroom.

Examples of Classroom Reading Inquiries			
Phase	Process	Engagement Inquiry Example	Feedback Inquiry Example
Pose and reflect	Set an intention for the inquiry by posing a question. Uncover what children already know and think about the question by engaging in reflective talk.	*What is engagement?* "I want us to come together to think about a question today. What does it mean to be engaged as a reader? What is engagement?"	*What is feedback?* "Every day we talk together as readers. In conferences especially, I am giving you feedback about what you are doing as a reader. What do you think feedback is? What do you already know about feedback?"
Explore next steps	Based on the strengths that emerge during reflection, ask the questions in the next column or provide next-steps feedback to grow the class' understanding further. Use these questions as a starting point, and develop different questions in response to the students.	Listen in to student reflections and pose the following questions, building on what students already know: • What does it feel like to be an engaged reader? • What are the habits of engaged readers? • How can book choice help us to be engaged? • How do we know when we are disengaged? • What can we do when we are disengaged?	Listen in to student reflections and pose the following questions, building on what students already know: • What does feedback sound like? What are different kinds of feedback? • How do I give my teacher feedback or talk about how my reading is going? • What do I do when my teacher gives me feedback? • How do I keep track of what I am doing?
Reflect	Take time to make the inquiry visible and lasting.	Ask, "What do we know now about engagement?" Create a class definition or chart to take the class' understandings public.	Ask, "What do we know now about feedback?" Create a class definition or chart to take the class' understandings public.

Using Read-Alouds as Entry Points

The read-aloud and independent reading are closely connected, informing and supporting one another across the school year. When we gather together to share a text, not only are we able to address timely topics and ideas, but we also provide the opportunity to spark ideas for new intentions. Carefully select texts to read aloud with two questions in mind: What might be the entry point for students? and What is our intended purpose for reading these texts? (Laminack and Kelly 2019). All read-alouds help build community, support engagement, inspire authentic student talk, and reinforce that reading is about meaning making. While you may select a text with one purpose for reading in mind, each student brings their own network of experiences that will ultimately influence their meaning making and interpretations.

When we read aloud for a variety of purposes, we open up space for the read-aloud to move around in our schedules as needed. There is no one place for read-aloud to live; rather we can make intentional decisions about the optimal timing within our daily schedule. You can use it to gather everyone together after lunch or as an ideal way to end the day, or you can integrate it into content areas. When independent reading is a vital part of classroom life, the read-aloud and the work of readers expand, fitting in with the work of writers, mathematicians, social comprehension, and content area instruction.

Here, we provide four varied purposes for selected read-alouds as a guide to think about providing multiple entry points for students as well as to expand the range of conversations that are possible in response to text. The texts we select and the meanings students construct from these texts may inspire other interpretations and lead to different intentions for each student. Making the conversation revolve around the teacher's purpose for choosing that book is not the goal. Rather, we choose read-alouds to create a variety of entry points for children as they make meaning from text while facilitating rich conversation.

Purpose **One**: To Make Texts Familiar

As caregivers and kindergarten teachers know, when we read the same book multiple times, children will soon pick up that book and read it themselves, relying on their memories and meaning-making ability. Children are attracted to familiar books, and familiar books breed comfort, enthusiasm, and confidence (Collins and Glover 2015). In lower-elementary classrooms, the work of making texts familiar is often done through shared repeated readings (Sulzby 1985). Teachers select a particular book and deliberately read it a number of times in a row across a week. Then teachers make multiple copies available to the students and encourage students to give the book a go on their own. Often, students don't even need explicit encouragement; familiar favorites fly off the shelves! While this example tends to resonate more soundly with lower-grade teachers, upper-grade teachers can also support their students' independent reading by selecting texts with the intention of making a series or genre more familiar and thus accessible.

Purpose **Two**: To Validate All Readers

One unintended consequence of choosing beautiful, complex picture books and challenging, thought-provoking novels as read-alouds is that it sends the message that these are the only kinds of texts that we value. Instead, we want to clearly send the message that we value all texts. We also want to be mindful of the books that students are reading independently. Put plainly, we want our students who are reading books that are less complex than their peers to feel valued. We can use the read-aloud to validate the levels and types of books that all students are reading. This means you might select read-alouds that represent a wide range of complexity, such as titles from a guided reading set, or you might read a graphic novel or other text outside of your comfort zone.

Purpose **Three**: To Inspire Readers

One surefire way to inspire readers who currently struggle with book choice is to pick books with those students in mind. The read-aloud can hook and inspire students. Once we have learned more about what the student is interested in, we can read books aloud that are based on their interests. We can curate text sets for them and read a few of those aloud.

We can also use the read-aloud to expand students' book choice by paying attention to what they are not choosing to read. For example, in many classrooms, fiction dominates during independent reading. We can read into students' gaps in book choices by selecting snappy informational texts to read aloud. We can inspire readers by noticing, naming, and promoting under-utilized sections of the classroom library through the read-aloud.

Finally, when selecting read-alouds with the intention of inspiring readers, it is always helpful to have something new in your back pocket. Paying attention to students' favorite authors, showcasing new series that have just come out, and creating excitement around newly nominated award contenders are all ways to build the sort of buzz that can capture the attention of all readers.

Purpose **Four**: To Reflect a Multitude of Identities and Cultivate Empathy

One way to make sure that our students are seen and valued is to read aloud from books in which they see themselves reflected. When students are seen and valued, they are more likely to feel connected to reading. Reading books that represent a range of experiences and choices also spurs students to construct and reconstruct their own identities, providing them with valuable ways to think about who they are in the world (Cherry-Paul and Johansen 2019).

Books are also a way for children to learn about people whose lives differ from theirs. In this case, the conversations sparked by read-alouds can be opportunities to cultivate empathy and to deepen students'—and our own—social comprehension (Ahmed 2018). Picking books that represent a variety of races, neighborhoods, homes, religions, cultures, family structure, experiences, and languages ensure that all students feel seen in the read-aloud. We also want to widen children's experiences so that they become aware of a reality that is not theirs and can develop empathy for others. When doing this, be sure to read books that include a variety of experiences, both extraordinary and ordinary.

The following chart illustrates how varying your intentions for read-alouds can inspire a wide range of student intentions.

How the Read-Aloud Can Inspire Student Intentions	
Read-Aloud Purpose	**Student Intentions It Might Inspire**
To make texts familiar	What if I reread my favorite books? What if I reread all the class read-alouds? What if I read everything by a familiar author?
To validate all readers	What if I read with a new partner? What if I found a lot to talk about in my books? What if I trusted myself to try something more challenging? What if I wanted to read only the pictures?
To inspire readers	What if I tried fantasy [a new genre]? What if I read a new series? What if I tried books by a new author? What if I read only online?
To reflect a multitude of identities and cultivate empathy	What if I found books with characters who reminded me of myself? What if I created a collection of books that represented me? What if I read books to learn about people who have had different experiences than my own? What if I read to find a way to create change? What if I read to imagine a better way?

The Cycle of Conferring
Across the Year

The Cycle of Conferring is designed to be flexible and responsive to the needs of your students as they grow throughout the school year. Students will go through multiple cycles during the school year. You will guide each student through these multiple cycles, adjusting the questions as needed. For example, at the beginning of the school year the Discovery Conference is framed by the question, Who are you as a reader? In subsequent Discovery Conferences, you might ask slightly different questions: Who are you as a reader now? How have you changed as a reader? How have read-alouds helped you? You might then include these subsequent prompts: Tell me about your what-if questions. Tell me about your most recent favorites. Tell me about your engagement in reading now. These questions and prompts encourage the student to reflect on their growth and find new intentions. As always, end the Discovery Conference by naming a strength related to the student's identity.

Similarly, students' intentions across the year naturally evolve and, as a result, so should your Intention Conferences. Keep track of students' intentions as a way to not only capture the skills and strategies embedded but also get a larger sense of how your readers enter into meaning making.

Practically speaking, we cannot name a specific number of cycles a child should engage in each year. Ideally, several. Typically, as children develop as readers, their intentions deepen and evolve as well and we want every child to have the opportunity to reflect upon a body of reading work.

When introducing the Cycle of Conferring to our youngest readers or to readers who are simply new to this experience, begin with a round of Discovery Conferences. Then, brainstorm possible intentions as a group. Determine which intentions spark the most curiosity or interest and then offer a menu of possibilities. Students can sign up to pursue an intention, creating a group. In this way, you can scaffold the group through the experience, providing students with beneficial opportunities to grow their talk and share ideas as well as more specific knowledge of what the cycle might look like individually.

In addition to being responsive to the needs of students, the cycle is responsive to other demands on your time, such as schoolwide periods of assessment. Many schools conduct formal benchmark assessments three times a year—in the fall, winter, and spring. Often, these assessments are administered during independent reading time, making it challenging to confer at the same time. Benchmark assessments yield important data that will inform your conferring work. Here are a few suggestions for how you can keep the Cycle of Conferring going and to make this big data collection feel like a seamless part of your instructional year:

- Conduct a round of Discovery Conferences, then administer your benchmark assessment prior to the Intention Conferences.

- Conduct the Discovery Conference right before diving into the benchmark assessment with each child.

- Spread your assessing out across the entire window. Stagger your start times with groups of students. Perhaps six students have a Discovery Conference and benchmark assessment one week and then move into Intention and Impact Conferences. Six students start the next week, and so on. This allows you to weave formal assessment into classroom practice, keeping your natural flow going and making tackling this task feel more manageable.

Considering Daily Schedules

Each school day is a new opportunity to craft a set of experiences for your readers based on your growing understanding of their identities, intentions, and needs. That being said, there is no one magical schedule that will work in all circumstances with all children. The following are a few tips for prioritizing what you value as you create a schedule that works for both you and your students:

- Think about whether you are allocating enough time to those experiences that have an instructional impact.

- Analyze your day minute by minute. Start by adding independent reading minutes; don't leave independent reading minutes for the leftovers. Eliminate time wasters. What is in the way of making time for impactful practices?

- If necessary, advocate for creating your own schedule and for having flexibility in your schedule. By modeling agency in this way, we are creating more space for our students to act with agency themselves. Support your position with research.

- Be flexible. Reading instruction does not have to go the same way every day. Looking across the week, instead of just each day, can often open up possibilities for balance. For more about how flexibility in reading might work, see Debbie Miller's *What's the Best That Could Happen?* (2019).

Considering Conferring Schedules

No one can create the perfect conferring schedule for you and your students. Once you have committed to devoting time to conferring, the schedules are mostly about math; you have a certain number of minutes for independent reading (a lot, we hope) and then you plug in the number of conferences and check-ins you can fit within that period of time. Be kind to yourself; scheduling every single minute does not allow for a moment of reflection and note-taking after a conference; nor does it feel good when the schedule becomes this impossible dream you must wrangle daily.

Your goal is to meet with every reader each week through a combination of conferences or small-group instruction. Each grade level presents its own considerations; here are some thoughts about specific grade-level bands:

- *Kindergarten:* Kindergarten is a unique and lovely time that does not necessarily lend itself to a great deal of independence right from the start! Independent reading at the beginning of the year is more of a joyful exploration of books, habits, sharing, and talk than it is a period of sustained quiet practice. Conferring at this time may consist of table conferences, in which you talk with a group of students sitting at the same table, rather than individual students, using the questions from the Discovery Conference as a guide for your conversation. The types of questions included in a Discovery Conference may be unfamiliar to some students; therefore, not only is talking about them in a small group more practical at this point in the year, but it also allows students to grow their talk together in response to these questions. In a small group, you'll be better positioned to provide models, sentence starters, or coach talk.

- Use your time early in the year to layer in the larger inquiry work and read-aloud experiences described here that will scaffold students to be more successful with the Cycle of Conferring later in the year. Formal use of the Cycle of Conferring may not begin until January, when students are better equipped to read for longer stretches of time.

- *Grade one:* The beginning of first grade may mirror the kindergarten experience as you set expectations for independent reading and build a culture that supports this conferring work. As always, trust yourself and follow the lead of your students, creating reading experiences that are responsive to their needs.

- *Grades two through five:* If students have spent several years in classrooms that prioritized independent reading, students will come to the upper-elementary grades with more stamina and experience with conferring. For students who may not have had previous opportunities for robust independent reading, start with building trusting relationships, rely on strategic whole-class inquiries about conferring, or create partnerships in which a child who has more experience with conferring can model and support their peer.

The Complete Cycle of Conferring: Two Stories

Here are two stories of students and the instructional possibilities that opened up when we found space for them to follow their own intentions as readers. Through independent reading and conferring across the year, these students pursued a number of what-if inquiries that led them to new understandings, including key reading skills and strategies, an expansion of their reading identity, word solving, vocabulary, theme and message, and building community through books.

A First Grader's Story

Meet Maria, a buoyant first grader. During her Discovery Conference, she shared everything from her favorite reading spot to the details of her upcoming sixth birthday party. We learned that Maria loved to read about trucks, confidently selected books from the classroom library based on her interests, and preferred to read by herself both at school and at home. She spent a lot of time "noticing the words" in books, and she read and reread books, practicing them until she felt confident. After reading a few pages with Maria, we realized that when she said that she was "noticing the words," she was actually confidently but repeatedly calling upon the same decoding strategy of looking at the initial sound along with using information from the picture. When Maria paused in her reading, we asked her to share what she was thinking. We learned that in addition to strategy work, Maria was also monitoring for meaning by checking to see if the word made sense in the larger sentence. We closed the conference by naming her strengths: "Maria, you are the kind of reader who pays attention to words in lots of ways. You are paying attention to the sounds that make up words, and you're also paying attention to which word makes sense inside the whole sentence."

In the Intention Conference, Maria reiterated that the reading process was her entry point for meaning making. When asked, "What do you want as a reader?" she answered, "I want to be able to read the words in the books that I like." Later in the conference, she shared that she felt she could accomplish this by "practicing and practicing bigger words." The next page shows the intention form we created alongside Maria to capture her

intention turned into a what-if
question and to serve as an
artifact to focus her purpose
for independent reading. We
ended the Intention Conference by reminding Maria of
her strong use of the initial
sound to solve words.

We began preparing by
reflecting on Maria's chosen
entry point: the reading
process. Building off her
strength, we decided to
introduce a variety of strategies for word solving appropriate to the level of texts
she was reading. Analyzing
prior running records, we noticed that Maria also appealed to the teacher for several
high-frequency words, so we included high-frequency words as another opportunity
for growth. We then moved to consider other entry points for meaning making. Maria's
strong sense of book choice was a strength; we determined what might be helpful next
would be to widen her book choice to think about fictional reading preferences as well.
Finally, in thinking about possibilities related to reading response, we wondered if
working alongside a group of readers to talk about word solving might inspire Maria to
transfer additional reading strategies.

Through four Impact Conferences, we were able to follow Maria's lead as she continued to enjoy books about trucks. By extending invitations to find new ways to solve
words, we were able to model and coach into several new strategies for Maria to use
independently. Maria decided to capture these strategies through pictures on a bookmark.
She noticed that she was not the only student who needed support with what she called
"tricky words" and thought her bookmark might also help others in the class. With a
small group of students, Maria led a conversation about her work with new strategies for
word solving and proudly gave copies of the bookmark to each person.

In our next conference, after working within her intention for two weeks, we did
a quick running record with Maria. Maria confidently used a wide range of strategies
appropriate for the complexity of text. She was ready to move on to a new intention.

We began again with a new Discovery Conference to get a better sense of how Maria
understood herself as a reader *now*. In response to a recent author study in read-aloud,
Maria said she was interested in reading more from that author, a shift that would

expand her reading identity to incorporate more fiction. We wondered aloud what would happen if she read a series of books by the same author, and a new intention was born. Maria was off and running with a new desire to tackle a fictional series, opening up new possibilities to transfer skills across genres and address new skills related to the reading of stories.

Here are some of Maria's first grade what-if questions:

- What if I practiced reading the words?
- What if I read all the books written by a favorite author?
- What if I followed a character across books?
- What if I learned lessons with my character?
- What if I read a lot of books about the same topic?

A Fourth Grader's Story

During the first Discovery Conference, Jason, a fourth-grade student, eagerly shared that he loved the character of Strega Nona, the I Survived series, and sports. Jason explained that he preferred informational texts, particularly those about endangered animals. He picked a nonfiction book about jaguars to read aloud, and he applied a variety of strategies when encountering challenging vocabulary. In discussing the text, Jason was able to synthesize it, even critiquing the use of headings. Next, we asked Jason to say more about his love of Strega Nona, as it is not every day you hear a fourth grader proclaim their love for this character. This tidbit stood out as a unique piece to Jason's reading identity . . . plus his face just lit up at the sound of her name. He told us that he actually loved picture books, particularly those books where the character learned a lesson. He laughed out loud when talking about Big Anthony's foibles.

After Jason returned to his independent reading, we reflected on what we had uncovered about his identity as a reader. Jason was clearly engaged in reading, using his specific interests to navigate book choices and showing an ability to read with a high level of understanding in nonfiction. We returned to his love of picture books; this was an interesting highlight to our conference that stood out as a unique aspect of Jason's identity. We began to grow a theory that we could build on this interest and encourage Jason to tackle longer and more complex fiction texts with the same savvy he showed when reading nonfiction.

When we met for the Intention Conference, Jason explained he now was working on figuring out harder words by looking for root words. We wondered about this, as it did not fit in with what he had discussed previously. From his running record and our informal observations, we knew that Jason was already flexibly using a variety of strategies for decoding words with a great deal of success. At that time, the class was currently studying root words during word study. Was this an example of a child being compliant and saying what he assumed teachers would want to hear?

With this in mind, we reiterated that he was in charge of what he wanted to focus on. He looked relieved, and said: "Strega Nona!" With Jason, we outlined three options:

1. What if we tried to identify the lessons learned from following our favorite characters?

2. What if we read to find another character to love?

3. What if we shared his love of Strega Nona books with others?

Jason connected with the first idea and suggested he could write the lesson learned on a sticky note and stick it to the front of each book for his friends to consider.

We began our preparing after the conference, beginning with the entry point of the reading process. In teacher talk, Jason was interested in studying character change over time so that he could infer the lesson learned by the character and then shift to critique how these lessons might be generalized. Jason exhibited strength when it came to analyzing character, so we decided that shifting to how those lessons might apply to his own life was a starting point. We then moved to consider possibilities for identity work by starting with his love of Tomie dePaola and working together to branch out to include other authors or series. Finally, we considered building community, noting Jason's desire to put lessons into writing. Through our kidwatching, we had previously noted that Jason was often reluctant to take a risk with the whole group, opting instead to share his thinking with a partner only. We began to think about the possibility of building on his talk to share his thinking about lessons with the class.

Over the course of six Impact Conferences, we met with Jason to learn more about how he determined the lesson in each story. Building on his strength, studying the problem and solution, we found space to coach Jason in other strategies for determining the lesson or message in a fictional text as well as how he might take a character's lesson and generalize it to his own life. In our final Impact Conference, Jason began to wonder if there were other stories in the classroom library that so clearly taught the reader a lesson. As a contribution to the class, he began a basket called "Life Lessons" to share. Included in the basket were all the Strega Nona books he had read, complete with lesson sticky notes on the cover. While introducing his basket, he invited other students to add books they discovered.

We kicked off a new cycle alongside Jason, returning to the Discovery Conference to gain insight into his current thinking as a reader. During this conference, Jason shared that he wanted to learn more about Italy, as it seemed to be such an important piece of the Strega Nona series. Here are a few of the intentions-turned-what-if-questions Jason tackled that year:

- What if I read to learn all about Italy?
- What if I read to learn about a variety of countries?
- What if I paid close attention to the setting?
- What if I figured out what new words really meant?
- What if I found books that I connected to the way I connect to Strega Nona?

Off You Go: Final Thoughts

Creating space for joyful independent reading and impactful conferring requires trust. Take a moment to reflect. What are your strengths? What are the strengths of your students? What are the strengths of your current independent reading and conferring practices? Name and celebrate your and your students' strengths.

Teaching is a daunting, demanding, engaging, and joyful job. We are responsible for apprenticing children into humanity and apprenticing them in ways that will sustain humanity itself (Johnston et al. 2020). We imagine school as a place of compassion, where students can know themselves, celebrate themselves, and get to know and celebrate others. If we approach this responsibility by teaching reading in transformative ways, we need to create spaces in which both we and our students trust our reading work.

As teachers, some of our most essential work is to imagine possibilities in the midst of all the demands on our time. By harnessing the power of social imagination (Greene 1995), teachers are able to imagine and pursue what *ought* to be, rather than feel compelled to work within current racial, social, and academic inequities. Our vision of what ought to be is one where schools educate all students equitably and honor the identities of all students.

And now what is next for you? What if you trust your readers?

Works Cited

Ahmed, Sara K. 2018. *Being the Change: Lessons and Strategies to Teach Social Comprehension* Portsmouth, NH: Heinemann.

Allen, Patrick A. 2009. *Conferring: The Keystone of Reader's Workshop*. Portland, ME: Stenhouse.

Allington, Richard L. 2012. *What Really Matters for Struggling Readers: Designing Research-Based Programs*. 3rd ed. New York: Pearson.

———. 2013. "What Really Matters When Working with Struggling Readers." *The Reading Teacher* 66 (7): 520–30.

———. 2014. "How Reading Volume Affects Both Reading Fluency and Reading Achievement." *International Electronic Journal of Elementary Education* 7 (1): 95–104. www.iejee.com/index .php/IEJEE/article/view/61/59.

Allington, Richard L., and Rachael E. Gabriel. 2012. "Every Child Every Day." *Educational Leadership* 69 (6): 10–15.

American Journal of Play. 2011. "Play and the Hundred Languages of Children: An Interview with Lella Gandini." *American Journal of Play* 4 (1): 1–18. www.journalofplay.org/sites /www.journalofplay.org/files/pdf-articles/4-1-interview-gandini.pdf.

Anderson, Carl. 2018. *A Teacher's Guide to Writing Conferences*. Portsmouth, NH: Heinemann.

———. 2000. *How's It Going? A Practical Guide to Conferring with Student Writers*. Portsmouth, NH: Heinemann.

APA Dictionary of Psychology. 2020. s.v. "trust." Accessed September 10, 2019. https://dictionary .apa.org/trust.

ASCD. 2020. "Whole Child." ASCD (website). www.ascd.org/whole-child.aspx.

Backman, Jill. 2016. "A Level Is a Teacher's Tool, NOT a Child's Label." *Fountas and Pinnell Literacy* (blog), September 29. https://fpblog.fountasandpinnell.com/a-level-is-a-teacher-s-tool -not-a-child-s-label.

Barnhouse, Dorothy. 2014. *Readers Front and Center: Helping All Students Engage with Complex Texts*. Portland, ME: Stenhouse.

Berger, Warren. 2014. *A More Beautiful Question: The Power of Inquiry to Spark Breakthrough Ideas*. New York: Bloomsbury.

Bishop, Rudine Sims. 1990. "Mirrors, Windows, and Sliding Glass Doors." *Perspectives: Choosing and Using Books for the Classroom* 6 (3): ix–xi.

Bryant, Adam. 2019. "How to Be a Better Listener." *New York Times*, March 4. https://www.nytimes .com/guides/smarterliving/be-a-better-listener.

Burkins, Jan, and Kim Yaris. 2014. *Who's Doing the Work? How to Say Less So Readers Can Do More*. Portland, ME: Stenhouse.

———. 2019. "Non-Judgmental Relentlessness." *Burkins and Yaris* (blog). www.burkinsandyaris.com /non-judgmental-relentlessness. Accessed August 5, 2019.

Calkins, Lucy M. 2001. *The Art of Teaching Reading*. Boston: Addison-Wesley.

Calkins, Lucy, and the Teachers College Reading and Writing Project. 2015. *A Guide to the Reading Workshop: Primary Grades*. Portsmouth, NH: Heinemann.

Cherry-Paul, Sonja, and Dana Johansen. 2019. *Breathing New Life into Book Clubs: A Practical Guide for Teachers*. Portsmouth, NH: Heinemann.

Clay, Marie M. 2005. *Literacy Lessons Designed for Individuals, Part One: Why? When? And How?* Portsmouth, NH: Heinemann.

Collins, Kathy, and Matt Glover. 2015. *I Am Reading: Nurturing Young Children's Meaning Making and Joyful Engagement with Any Book*. Portsmouth, NH: Heinemann.

Comer, James P. 1980. *School Power: Implications of an Intervention Project*. New York: Teachers College Press.

Cooperative Children's Book Center. 2020. School of Education, University of Wisconsin-Madison. https://ccbc.education.wisc.edu/literature-resources/ccbc-diversity-statistics/books-by -about-poc-fnn/. Accessed November 1, 2020.

Dinnerstein, Renee. 2016. *Choice Time: How to Deepen Learning Through Inquiry and Play*. Portsmouth, NH: Heinemann.

Dotlich, Rebecca Kai. 2019. *What If . . . ? Then We . . . : Short, Very Short, Shorter-than-Ever Possibilities*. Honesdale, PA: Boyds Mills Press.

Eakins, Sheldon. 2020. *Getting Started with Educational Equity: Ten Steps to Get You on the Right Path Towards Leading Equity*. Pocatello, ID: Leading Equity. https://arkansasstemcoalition.com /wp-content/uploads/2020/07/UAMhwF9rSse4pvAJyOuu_Getting_Started_with _Educational_Equity.pdf.

Eberhardt, Jennifer. 2019. "What Police Departments and the Rest of Us Can Do to Overcome Implicit Bias, According to an Expert." Interview by Belinda Luscombe. *Time*, March 27. https://time.com/5558181/jennifer-eberhardt-overcoming-implicit-bias/.

España, Carla, and Luz Y. Herrera. 2020. *En comunidad: Lessons for Centering the Voice and Experiences of Bilingual Latinx Students*. Portsmouth, NH: Heinemann.

Fisher, Douglas, Nancy Frey, and Nancy Akhavan. 2019. *This Is Balanced Literacy, Grades K–6*. Thousand Oaks, CA: Corwin Literacy.

Fisher, Douglas, Nancy Frey, and Russell J. Quaglia. 2018. *Engagement by Design: Creating Learning Environments Where Students Thrive*. Thousand Oaks, CA: Corwin Literacy.

Förster, Natalie, and Elmar Souvignier. 2014. "Learning Progress Assessment and Goal Setting: Effects on Reading Achievement, Reading Motivation and Reading Self-Concept." *Learning and Instruction* 32: 91–100.

Fountas, Irene C., and Gay Su Pinnell. 2017. *The Fountas and Pinnell Literacy Continuum: A Tool for Assessment, Planning, and Teaching*. Portsmouth, NH: Heinemann.

———. 2019. "Level Books, Not Children: The Role of Text Levels in Literacy Instruction." Fountas and Pinnell Literacy. www.fountasandpinnell.com/shared/resources/FPL _LevelBooksNotKids_Whitepaper.pdf.

Frazin, Shana, and Katy Wischow. 2019. *Unlocking the Power of Classroom Talk: Teaching Kids to Talk with Clarity and Purpose*. Portsmouth, NH: Heinemann.

Goldberg, Gravity. 2016. *Mindsets and Moves: Strategies That Help Readers Take Charge, Grades 1–8*. Thousand Oaks, CA: Corwin Literacy.

Greene, Maxine. 1995. *Releasing the Imagination: Essays on Education, the Arts and Social Change*. San Francisco: Jossey-Bass.

Guthrie, John, and Allan Wigfield. 2000. "Engagement and Motivation in Reading." In *Handbook of Reading Research*, vol. 3, ed. Michael L. Kamil, Peter B. Mosenthal, P. David Pearson, and Rebecca Barr, 403–22. Mahwah, NJ: Earlbaum.

Hall, Leigh A. 2007. "Understanding the Silence: Struggling Readers Discuss Decisions About Reading Expository Text." *Journal of Educational Research* 100 (3): 132–41.

———. 2012. "The Role of Reading Identities and Reading Abilities in Students' Discussions About Texts and Comprehension Strategies." *Journal of Literacy Research* 44 (3): 239–72.

Hamilton, L., Halverson, R., Jackson, S., Mandinach, E., Supovitz, J., and Wayman, J. (2009). *Using Student Achievement Data to Support Instructional Decision Making* (NCEE 2009-4067). Washington, DC: National Center for Education Evaluation and Regional Assistance, Institute of Education Sciences, U.S. Department of Education. Retrieved from http://ies .ed.gov/ncee/wwc/publications/practiceguides/.

Hattie, John. 2012. *Visible Learning for Teachers: Maximizing Impact on Learning*. London and New York: Routledge.

Hattie, John, and Shirley Clarke. 2019. *Visible Learning: Feedback*. London and New York: Routledge.

Hernandez, Donald J. 2012. *Double Jeopardy: How Third-Grade Reading Skills and Poverty Influence High School Graduation*. Baltimore, MD: Annie E. Casey Foundation. www.aecf.org/ resources/double-jeopardy/.

Hertz, Christine, and Kristine Mraz. 2018. *Kids 1st from Day 1: A Teacher's Guide to Today's Classroom*. Portsmouth, NH: Heinemann.

Hollie, Sharrokey. 2018. *Culturally and Linguistically Responsive Teaching and Learning: Classroom Practices for Student Success*. Huntington Beach, CA: Shell Education.

Howard, Jaleel R., Tanya Milner-McCall, and Tyrone C. Howard. 2020. *No More Teaching Without Positive Relationships*. Portsmouth, NH: Heinemann.

International Literacy Association (ILA). 2018. *Literacy Leadership Brief: The Power and Promise of Read-Alouds and Independent Reading*. No. 9445. Newark, DE: Author. https:// literacyworldwide.org/docs/default-source/where-we-stand/ila-power-promise-read-alouds-independent-reading.pdf.

———. 2020. "Children's Rights to Read." International Literacy Association (website). https: //literacyworldwide.org/docs/default-source/resource-documents/ila-childrens-rights-to -read.pdf.

Johnston, Peter H. 2004. *Choice Words: How Our Language Affects Children's Learning*. Portland, ME: Stenhouse.

———. 2012. *Opening Minds: Using Language to Change Lives*. Portland, ME: Stenhouse.

Johnston, Peter H., Kathy Champeau, Andrea Hartwig, Sarah Helmer, Merry Komar, Tara Krueger, and Laurie McCarthy. 2020. *Engaging Literate Minds: Developing Children's Social, Emotional and Intellectual Lives, K–3*. Portsmouth, NH: Stenhouse.

Keene, Ellin O. 2018. *Engaging Children: Igniting a Drive for Deeper Learning, K–8*. Portsmouth, NH: Heinemann.

Kendi, Ibram X. 2019. *How to Be an Antiracist*. New York: One World.

Krashen, Stephen. 2004. *The Power of Reading: Insights from the Research*. Santa Barbara, CA: Libraries Unlimited.

Laminack, Lester, and Katie Kelly. 2019. *Reading to Make a Difference: Using Literature to Help Students Speak Freely, Think Deeply, and Take Action*. Portsmouth, NH: Heinemann.

Library of Congress. 2018. "Jacqueline Woodson Named Sixth National Ambassador for Young People's Literature." Library of Congress (website), January 4. www.loc.gov/item/prn-18-001.

Lingard, Bob, Debra Hayes, and Martin Mills. 2003. "Teachers and Productive Pedagogies: Contextualising, Conceptualising, Utilising." *Pedagogy, Culture, & Society* 11 (3): 399–424.

Locke, Edwin A., and Gary P. Latham. 2006. "New Directions in Goal-Setting Theory." *Current Directions in Psychological Science* 15 (5): 265–68.

Martinelli, Marjorie, and Kristine Mraz. 2012. *Smarter Charts, K–2: Optimizing an Instructional Staple to Create Independent Readers and Writers*. Portsmouth, NH: Heinemann.

Massaro, Dominic W. 2017. "Reading Aloud to Children: Benefits and Implications for Acquiring Literacy Before Schooling Begins." *The American Journal of Psychology* 130 (1): 63–72.

McTigue, Erin M., Erin K. Washburn, and Jeffrey Liew. 2009. "Academic Resilience and Reading: Building Successful Readers." *The Reading Teacher* 62 (5): 422–32.

Merriam-Webster. 2019. s.v. "problem." Accessed September 10, 2019. www.merriam-webster.com/dictionary/problem.

Miller, Debbie. 2019. *What's the Best That Could Happen? New Possibilities for Teachers and Readers*. Portsmouth, NH: Heinemann.

Miller, Debbie, and Barbara Moss. 2013. *No More Independent Reading Without Support*. Portsmouth, NH: Heinemann.

Miller, Donalyn. 2009. *The Book Whisperer: Awakening the Inner Reader in Every Child*. San Francisco: Jossey-Bass.

Minor, Cornelius. 2019. *We Got This: Equity, Access, and the Quest to Be Who Our Students Need Us to Be*. Portsmouth, NH: Heinemann.

Muhammad, Gholdy. 2020. *Cultivating Genius: An Equity Framework for Culturally Responsive and Historically Responsive Literacy*. New York: Scholastic.

Mulligan, Tammy, and Clare Landrigan. 2018. *It's All About the Books: How to Create Bookrooms and Classroom Libraries That Inspire Readers*. Portsmouth, NH: Heinemann.

———. 2019. "Top Ten Book Basket Labels Created by Kids." *The Nerdy Book Club* (blog), March 30. https://nerdybookclub.wordpress.com/2019/03/30/top-ten-book-basket-labels -created-by-kids-by-tammy-mulligan-and-clare-landrigan/.

Murdoch, Kath. 2015. *The Power of Inquiry: Teaching and Learning with Curiosity, Creativity and Purpose in the Contemporary Classroom.* Melbourne, Australia: Seastar Education Consulting.

National Council of Teachers of English (NCTE). 2019. "Statement on Independent Reading." NCTE (website), November 7. https://ncte.org/statement/independent-reading/.

National Education Association. 2016. *Backgrounder: Students from Poverty.* Washington, DC: Author. www.useaut.org/assets/docs/Backgrounder_Students%20from%20poverty_online.pdf.

Nichols, Maria. 2019. *Building Bigger Ideas: A Process for Teaching Purposeful Talk.* Portsmouth, NH: Heinemann.

Nuthall, Graham. 2007. *The Hidden Lives of Learners.* Wellington, New Zealand: NZCER Press.

Owocki Gretchen, and Yetta Goodman. 2002. *Kidwatching: Documenting Children's Literacy Development.* Portsmouth, NH: Heinemann.

Parker, Kimberly. 2017. "Centering the Literacy Lives of Young People of Color in Our Classrooms: Reaching the Brilliant and the Bored." *Heinemann Professional Development Catalog-Journal 2017,* 54–55. www.heinemann.com/pd/journal/2017/parker_reaching _brilliant_and_bored.pdf.

Parks, Brenda. 1999. *Read It Again! Revisiting Shared Reading.* Portland, ME: Stenhouse.

Perie, Marianne, Wendy S. Grigg, and Patricia L. Donahue. (2005). *The Nation's Report Card: Reading 2005* (NCES 2006–451). U.S. Department of Education, Institute of Education Sciences, National Center for Education Statistics. Washington, DC: U.S. Government Printing Office. Retrieved from https://nces.ed.gov/nationsreportcard/pdf /main2005/2006451.pdf.

Purkey, William Watson, and John M. Novak. 1996. *Inviting School Success: A Self-Concept Approach to Teaching, Learning and Democratic Practice.* 3rd ed. Belmont, CA: Wadsworth.

Renzulli, Joseph S. 2008. "Engagement Is the Answer." *Education Week,* July 14. www.edweek.org /ew/articles/2008/07/16/43renzulli.h27.html.

Robinson, Sir Ken. 2017. *Out of Our Minds: The Power of Being Creative.* 3rd ed. Oxford, UK: Capstone.

Rosenblatt, Louise M. 1978. *The Reader, the Text, the Poem: The Transactional Theory of the Literary Work.* Carbondale, IL: Southern Illinois University Press.

Routman, Reggie. 2002. *Reading Essentials: The Specifics You Need to Teach Reading Well.* Portsmouth, NH: Heinemann.

———. 2018. *Literacy Essentials: Engagement, Excellence, and Equity for All Learners.* Portland, ME: Stenhouse.

Sahlberg, Pasi. 2017. "Big Data or Small Data: What's the Key to Unlocking Learning Opportunities?" *Pasi Sahlberg* (blog), May 5. https://pasisahlberg.com/big-data-or-small -data-whats-the-key-to-unlocking-learning-opportunities/.

Scholastic. 2019. *Kids and Family Reading Report*. 7th edition. Scholastic (website). www.scholastic
.com/readingreport/home.html.

Schunk, Dale. 2003. "Self-Efficacy for Reading and Writing: Influence of Modeling, Goal Setting, and Self-Evaluation." *Reading and Writing Quarterly* 19 (2): 159–72.

Serravallo, Jennifer. 2019. *Complete Comprehension: Fiction: Assessing, Evaluating, and Teaching to Support Students' Comprehension of Chapter Books*. Portsmouth, NH: Heinemann.

———. 2015. *The Reading Strategies Book: Your Everything Guide to Developing Skilled Readers*. Portsmouth, NH: Heinemann.

Staats, Cheryl, Kelly Capatosto, Lena Tenney, and Sarah Mamo. 2017. *State of the Science: Implicit Bias Review*. Columbus, OH: Kirwan Institute for the Study of Race and Ethnicity.

Sulzby, Elizabeth. 1985. "Children's Emergent Reading of Favorite Storybooks: A Developmental Study." *Reading Research Quarterly* 20 (4): 458–81.

Trelease, Jim. 2001. *The Read-Aloud Handbook*. New York: Penguin Books.

Wayman, Jeffrey C. 2005. "Involving Teachers in Data-Driven Decision Making: Using Computer Data Systems to Support Teacher Inquiry and Reflection." *Journal of Education for Students Placed at Risk* 10 (3): 295–308.

Wayman, Jeffrey C., Jo Beth Jimerson, and Vincent Cho. 2012. "Organizational Considerations in Establishing the Data-Informed District." *School Effectiveness and School Improvement* 23 (2): 159–78. www.researchgate.net/publication/233027295_Organizational_considerations
_in_establishing_the_Data-Informed_District.

We Need Diverse Books (website), accessed August 5, 2019, https://diversebooks.org.

Wiggins, Grant. 2013. "Genuine vs. Sham Accountability." *Granted and . . .* (blog), November 14. https://grantwiggins.wordpress.com/2013/11/14/genuine-vs-sham-accountability/.

Wiggins, Grant, and Jay McTighe. 2013. *Essential Questions: Opening Doors to Student Understanding*. Alexandria, VA: ASCD.

Wohlstetter, Priscilla, Amanda Datnow, and Vicki Park. 2008. "Creating a System of Data-Driven Decision-Making: Applying the Principal-Agent Framework." *School Effectiveness and School Improvement* 19 (3): 239–59. DOI:10.1080/09243450802246376.

Zak, Paul J. 2017. "The Neuroscience of Trust." *Harvard Business Review*, January–February. https://hbr.org/2017/01/the-neuroscience-of-trust.

Ziemke, Kristin, and Katie Muhtaris. 2019. *Read the World: Rethinking Literacy for Empathy and Action in a Digital Age*. Portsmouth, NH: Heinemann.